"Karoline Lewis once again demonstrates why she is one of the nation's preeminent preachers and pro_____ _____ _____ reaching.' Lewis's book beautifumilet-ics with sensitivity and pas ledge, the practitioner's depth, an f this often-misunderstood art for o the canon of homiletics and rhet__

—C _____ _____ _____ __ ___ᵣᵢnity United Church of Christ, and Professor of Homiletics, McAfee School of Theology, Mercer University

"Try to find another book like this. Ever the teacher, Lewis introduces preachers to a range of life-giving interpretive practices few mainline preachers know what to do with while modeling their usefulness. This book can bring joy and power to your preaching."

—**GREG CAREY,** Professor of New Testament, Lancaster Theological Seminary

"Just as diverse as the historical, cultural, and linguistic sources of the Bible are, so are the ways to interpret it. Karoline Lewis, the homiletical hermeneut, is an expert guide to the various approaches to biblical interpretation for the purpose of preaching. More than a summary of each approach and exploring its homiletical impact, Lewis offers readers a generous, humble reading of how 'the other' interprets Scripture to humanize those who have often been dehumanized in the wider society. I can think of no other better biblical scholar-preacher to invite us on this liberating tour of love for God, neighbor, and the pulpit."

—**LUKE A. POWERY,** Dean, Duke University Chapel, and Associate Professor of Homiletics, Duke Divinity School

"Karoline Lewis's clarity and warmth shine in her careful mapping of urgent conversations in the homiletic field. That alone is worth the price of admission. But the real treasure of *Preaching the Word* is the delight it takes in John's Gospel. Lewis turns the biblical text like a prism, showing us the value of the approaches that she describes through scriptural engagement. Her insights will keep me turning to this book again and again."

—**JERUSHA MATSEN NEAL,** Assistant Professor of Homiletics, Duke Divinity School

"As methods and approaches in biblical studies have proliferated, keeping up with all these developments is a full-time job! Karoline Lewis does not just summarize these emerging approaches for busy preachers. Instead, she models how preachers can learn from and be formed by these diverse approaches with care, thought, and respect. In these ways, preachers will find in this book a transformative path toward richer and more faithful proclamation of the gospel."

—**ERIC BARRETO,** Frederick and Margaret L. Weyerhaeuser
Associate Professor of New Testament,
Princeton Theological Seminary

"This timely book by seasoned preacher and homiletics professor (and Johannine scholar) Karoline Lewis will help preachers and seminary professors alike. The format of the book makes it easy to use. Each chapter introduces the reader to a particular approach in biblical interpretation that has arisen in the past fifteen years, uses a passage from John to illustrate the power of the approach to yield fresh insights, and connects it all with proclamation for those of us living in real bodies in the real world, a world marked by divinely designed diversity and the possibility of healing and hope. I especially appreciated her attention to trauma-informed interpretation and preaching, one of the newest approaches.

Lewis invites us into a conversation marked by humility and curiosity; she hopes that the first question asked when we finish the book is "Who else?" Whose voice is not reflected in the book? Rather than pronouncing the authoritative last word on the subject, she is cultivating in us a *habit* of always seeking to move beyond our own limited view and experience.

I wish I could share a number of my favorite quotes, but you will just have to dive in yourself. Allow me this one: "Having an open stance toward Scripture, listening to the many meanings it prompts, and reading decentered voices can renew the biblical and homiletical imagination of even the weariest preacher." Lewis's book will *energize* those who are weary, curious, or both."

—**JAIME CLARK-SOLES,** Professor of New Testament,
Perkins School of Theology, Southern Methodist University

Preaching the Word

Preaching the Word

*Contemporary Approaches
to the Bible for the Pulpit*

Karoline M. Lewis

WESTMINSTER
JOHN KNOX PRESS
LOUISVILLE • KENTUCKY

First edition
Published by Westminster John Knox Press
Louisville, Kentucky

23 24 25 26 27 28 29 30 31 32—10 9 8 7 6 5 4 3 2 1

Book design by Drew Stevens
Cover design by Leah Lococo

Library of Congress Cataloging-in-Publication Data is on file
at the Library of Congress, Washington, DC.

ISBN-13: 978-0-664-26662-2

Most Westminster John Knox Press books are available at special quantity discounts when purchased in bulk by corporations, organizations, and special-interest groups. For more information, please e-mail SpecialSales@wjkbooks.com.

For Gwen and Mike—
and our shared love of hermeneutics
over wine and good food

Contents

Acknowledgments

I am exceedingly grateful to Bob Ratcliff, Editor-in-Chief at Westminster John Knox Press, for the many conversations that led to the idea for this book, for his faith in me, and for his encouragement and support. I am also grateful to Luther Seminary for the yearlong sabbatical from teaching and other faculty responsibilities that made completing this book possible. A writing project never happens in isolation—for the goodwill and loving wishes of family and friends, I am so appreciative. Writing a book in the midst of a global pandemic meant a kind of authorial seclusion even beyond the usual isolation necessary for writing. I had to face what this book seeks to challenge—the quarantining of our ideas, the sequestration of our perspectives. The approaches outlined in this book pulled me outside of myself. They were not objects of study, but dialogue partners, saving me from our all-too-human tendency toward appropriation of our self-aggrandized thoughts. Rather than be the preacher, I became the listener, and heard God's Word anew. I hope the same for you, faithful readers, teachers, and preachers.

Karoline M. Lewis
Pentecost 2022

Introduction

This book invites preachers to consider how recent and various approaches in biblical interpretation, particularly those developed since the historical-critical method in which most clergy have been and are still trained, can have an immediate homiletical payoff. In general, it is challenging for preachers to keep up with developments in biblical scholarship, perhaps having not engaged further formal biblical study since their seminary days. Preaching courses, or classes in biblical studies for that matter, offered at mainline seminaries are not able to address fully either the history of biblical interpretation or the perspectives outlined in this volume. As required course work in practical theology continues to diminish, teachers of homiletics are left with one foundational preaching course, ensuring that continuing learning in biblical interpretation and method is essential for the faithful biblical preacher. Furthermore, seminary curricula typically are not consistent in helping students integrate biblical exegesis and biblical interpretation with a specific eye toward preaching.

The nature of this book points to a larger debate in biblical scholarship of "the relationship between *Wissenschaft* (primarily the historical-critical methodology) and contextual hermeneutics."[1] For the most part, preachers are still educated in the historical-critical method because it remains the controlling interpretive practice in biblical scholarship. The purpose of this book is not to contend for one approach over another or to pit interpretive methods against each other. Nor is the intent of this book to eschew the historical-critical method. Rather, the perspectives presented in the following chapters make evident that "the historical-critical approach is not able to answer all of the questions we bring to the texts as readers."[2] The approaches summarized below both complexify and humanize biblical interpretation, representing a stance toward the Bible especially critical for preaching: the Bible is not simply a source for a sermon but a dialogue partner in our own meaning making. "We engage texts as constructs of their own reality, in whatever time period and with whatever ideological strategy they employ. We will construct a new reality of that ancient reading, using the tools of history, the social sciences, and engaging the readings of others, including an investigation of their social location, ideological agendas, and otherness."[3]

Addressing how the Bible gets read is, in part, a responsibility of the preacher. The preaching task often demands corrective and truth telling, where the preacher calls out interpretations of biblical texts that have been harmful, hurtful, and erroneous because self-interpretation and contextuality have been neglected or ignored. It is likely that the majority of people in our ministry settings unknowingly employ historical criticism when reading Scripture, where "meaning exists in the world behind the text as something to be extracted or excavated and . . . the interpreter of the text is a neutral party, who, at her or his best, is able to maintain objectivity, promote positivism, and support universality."[4] Our listeners are prone to presume that a biblical passage holds one meaning, even though logically they also know that preachers would be out of jobs if that were indeed the case. At the same time, our faithful hearers have experienced the phenomenon of how a passage can have different meanings at various points in and passages of their lives but are not able to articulate why this holds true. Preaching should regularly point out and address these changing interpretations.

Another way to articulate the tension outlined above is to speak about reading and objectivity, regardless of whether it is the Bible being read. While historically "biblical scholarship valorized objectivity in interpretation," recent trends in biblical interpretation "foreground the contributions of culture, faith, and identity." Whereas the dominant approach sought to compartmentalize "race, ethnicity, nationality, global positioning, gender, class, sexual orientation, and physical ability," contemporary interpretation marks "the turn toward real flesh-and-blood readers" who bring "these dimensions of human experience to the forefront."[5] The more preaching honors the "flesh-and-blood" realities of our listeners, the more the faithful might see their contexts and locations as worthy of voice.

A cursory evaluation of preaching today exposes a general lack of biblical rigor, especially when it comes to evidence of engagement with approaches in biblical criticism beyond the historical-critical method. Conversations with preachers expose a dearth of continuing education in biblical interpretation and even shame around not keeping up with the latest trends in biblical studies. Rather than admit the need for further instruction, preachers continue their exegetical practices with minimal additional training, especially unaware of how developments in biblical scholarship are relevant for preaching. The hope is that with clear introductions to and applications of recent approaches in biblical interpretation, this book will demonstrate how these scholarly approaches make a difference for preaching and for ministry to and with the lives of faithful listeners.

The intention of this book is not simply to describe these approaches in biblical scholarship but also to establish how these approaches have significant homiletical impact. Knowing and using these approaches can make a marked difference in the quality and quantity of biblical presence in sermons, and this difference matters to the listeners. The preacher is accountable to the ways in which the Bible is heard and read, particularly outside of localized congregational comfort zones. How is the Bible interpreted by those beyond our immediate circle, congregation, and community? Preachers are also responsible for tending the biblical awareness of the congregation or community in which they do ministry. It is the preacher's job to bring communities of the faithful into dialogue with diverse interpreters of Scripture. Attention to trends in biblical scholarship can also address the perceived problem of biblical illiteracy in the church. Biblical illiteracy will not be solved by making sure our listeners know more about the Bible or have more information about theology. Rather, biblical literacy grows when the preacher models the reciprocity of Scripture and life. When current issues and approaches in biblical scholarship are taken seriously in preaching, the preacher gives witness to the open-ended ways in which God's people interact with God's Word. The hearers of our sermons have a better understanding of how the truths of our wide-ranging contexts make for a *living* Word.

WHY THIS BOOK

In a time when what the Bible says and means seems to be at the whim of the interpreter, it is critically important for the preacher to address the many viewpoints through which the Bible is read and interpreted. The reason is not only the homiletical consequence of such attention, but also pastoral concern. In our rapidly changing and challenging world, the faithful need to know that Scripture changes with the world; that the Bible is not a static document, but the living Word of God that continues to suggest new meanings of its age-old stories and for our lives. The focus of this book, therefore, is on the various cultural contexts that shape interpretation.

The sermon is never just information about God or what we are to understand about Jesus. The heart and soul of a sermon is an actual encounter with the living Christ, where the Word of God is reincarnated in the hearing and then embodied in the lives of the listeners. If preachers believe that the sermon is an event, then how they engage Scripture in the sermon should be demonstrative of this conviction. As a result, the Bible cannot merely be the subject matter of the sermon but that which animates and inspires listeners to engage in acts of interpretation. The best sermons invite the listeners to imagine that they themselves, like the voices they hear in the Bible, are worthy of contribution to the canon. While the canon may be closed, the diverse ways in which the Bible gets interpreted cannot be left to the so-called scholar alone. The preacher engages these different approaches in making sense of Scripture so that the listeners can see themselves as part of the conversation. As a result, interpreting the Bible becomes a dialogical process and listeners are then encouraged to believe that they are integral to such dialogue. There really is no sermon without their partnership in the conversation with the text.

Having a more generous stance to the varied approaches brought to the interpretation of the Bible also results in listeners being better readers of Scripture in general. Biblical preaching not only invites interpretive dialogue but also models nuance and dexterity in reading the Bible. Sermons are an act of empowerment, helping listeners embrace their own agency in meaning making, both of Scripture and of how God is working in their lives. Establishing that there are different approaches brought to the interpretation of Scripture, and that these approaches are valid, affirms that the listeners have a role in the interpretive enterprise.

Awareness of current trends in biblical interpretation also helps preachers grow in their own engagement with and trust in Scripture. The Bible is not simply the material on which sermons are based but bids new imagination about God and how God reveals God's self in the world. When preachers are more connected to Scripture and its diversity, they are better able to show how the Bible is an essential resource for making sense of our world, ourselves, and God's revelation to and in both.

As noted above, incorporating these varied approaches to interpreting the Bible into sermons communicates the multiple meanings that can be ascribed to a biblical passage. In theory, congregations and communities of faith might understand the multivalence of Scripture, and preachers suppose this truth simply by the fact that they preach manifold sermons on the same biblical passage and yet preach a different sermon each time around. At the same time, while preachers might be aware of this phenomenon, that awareness does not necessarily trickle down to the hearers. The more preachers can communicate *how* meaning happens, and that meaning changes depending on multiple issues, the more the hearers will be able to understand and navigate the many influences that shape how they interpret Scripture.

Intentional use of these different approaches in interpreting the Bible also functions as a critique of the hegemony of the white, male, cisgender, European representation in biblical scholarship. This hegemony means that the majority of the voices outlined in this book have yet to find any kind of mainstream attention in biblical interpretation. Instead, these approaches are still considered ideological, as if the dominant approach, the historical-critical method dictated by the authority of centuries of white, male perspectives, is free of bias. To put it another way,

> Precisely because perspective cannot be avoided, when it is not explicitly acknowledged the result is that a particular perspective takes on an aura of universality. Thus it happens that theology from a male perspective claims to be generally human, and that North Atlantic white theology believes itself to be "normal," while theologies from the so-called Third World or from ethnic minorities in the North Atlantic are taken to be contextual or perspectival.[6]

The truth is, "white interpreters have rarely reflected upon how culture and identity shape their own interpretive work." Because "whiteness" "does not function as an operative category," interpreters who are white seldom "grapple with their own race and ethnicity in public ways."[7] For hearers to experience liberation from officious interpretations, and those that have typically silenced marginalized voices, the voices "left out of the biblical interpretive enterprise,"[8] the preacher must engage these different approaches. As a result, the listeners might actually hear themselves in the pages of Scripture. From this stance, "the Bible is a democratizing book. It is a collection of writings spanning the G*d-experience of many centuries, a book in which a rich plurality of 'citizen' voices argue with each other, complement each other, and keep alive the vision of divine justice, care, and well-being."[9]

Finally, at stake is the way the church itself has been complicit in sidelining minoritized perspectives in its preaching and teaching. Responsible preachers reflect on the limitations of their tradition, denominational commitments, and creedal and confessional statements, and ask where and how these authorities come under regular scrutiny for the sake of inclusion, diversity, and equity in interpretive representation. For the preacher, then, "drawing closer to marginalized people requires, first, an attitude of humility."[10] It involves remembering that, for the most part, we occupy the center and that "to be marginal means to be excluded from the center."[11] Historically, systems of the church, such as synods, judicatories, councils, and sessions, have not tended the variances in biblical interpretation, likely to protect and maintain their ecclesial distinctiveness within Christianity. It is the charge of the preacher to challenge these embedded majority perspectives toward honest and unifying dialogue among Christian expressions and even toward interreligious conversations. The truth is, "the world of biblical interpretation includes all kinds of people. Real people."[12]

WHAT TO EXPECT

Each chapter of this book includes a brief introduction to an approach; a summary of the key issues and components of the approach; an engagement of the approach with a sample text, specifically a passage from the Gospel of John assigned by the Revised Common Lectionary; and a summary of homiletical implications for the craft of preaching, for effective church leadership, and for pastoral ministry. The chapters close with a list of further resources for engaging the approach, especially with a view toward preaching. A full bibliography concludes the book.

An important caveat is in order here. The presentations of the different approaches included in this book are by no means exhaustive of the field. Contributions are constantly being added, representing the complexities of the contexts reflected in the approaches. As a result, readers might also ask, "Where is Native American interpretation? Where is . . . ?" Good. That is one of the hoped-for results of this project. At the end, we should be left asking, "Who else?" While the approaches set forth in this volume are those that have taken hold in academic circles, as soon as this book is published, there will be other voices and perspectives that need to be heard. Perspectives chosen for this volume are those that have wider consequences for homiletics and ministry.

The preacher is called to speak about and from God's Word as it intersects with the various issues and concerns of our multifaceted contexts. Familiarity and engagement with these perspectives are necessary not only for the sake of faithful biblical interpretation but also for faithful pastoral ministry.

1

Literary/Narrative Approaches

INTRODUCTION

This first chapter focuses on literary approaches to biblical interpretation because these approaches represent the beginning steps toward dismantling the monopoly of the historical-critical method in biblical interpretation. The turn toward literary features of biblical texts, and thereby also how a reader responds, shifted the location of meaning for the interpretive enterprise. Whereas the historical-critical method situated meaning "behind" the text, or saw the text as "window," literary approaches look for meaning "in" the text. By analyzing literary dimensions, characters, dialogue, plot, setting, poetry, and prose, they seek to view the text as a work of art. "The turn to literary interpretation also sets us free to enjoy the Bible's many examples of literary artistry."[1] As we will see, this shift then leads to investigation of meaning "around" the text or "in front of the text," where the current readers' experience of the text is determined by intersectional contexts.

When literary theory showed up as a character in the play of biblical studies, the whole production seemed to demand a remake. The plot thickened. Unexpected twists and turns kept even the most engaged scholar off guard. A play turned into a miniseries that then became a serial drama. What happened?

The first thing to note is what literary theory is not—a "breath of fresh air" kind of approach that reads for the "fun stuff" about

Scripture, such as setting, plot, and character development, thereby evading the complex historicity of the text. This understanding is lodged as a caution to preachers who, in search of "that'll preach," leave the historical behind. Literary critics are not *anti-* or *a*historical.[2] Two other misunderstandings of New Testament literary criticism are worth mentioning, especially since these misrepresentations can lead to the oversimplification of literary theory and the New Testament: first, that literary theory is only interested in the final form of the text and that it is bent on guarding the "literariness" of the text, especially the author's literary expertise. Second, that a literary approach in biblical interpretation can be a standardized method. The literary features, forms, and genres found in the Bible are impossibly vast to homogenize.

A brief introduction is an oxymoron when it comes to literary interpretation of the Bible but will have to suffice for the purposes of this book. No one avenue of approach offered by literary theory can exhaust the literary potential of a text. Indeed, "while each form of literary criticism may be valid within its own frame of reference, none on its own can account for the full range of interpretive horizons engendered by a given literary text."[3] The field is broad, wide, and deep. Nor is any theory ever a panacea. A word of caution is appropriate here, especially for homiletical sensitivities toward texts: theoretical concepts are "*not* to be introduced for their own sake or to be nit-picked endlessly, but to be applied to texts. They should sharpen and enrich our interpretation of texts. At the same time, theory should never become a straightjacket . . . the function of theory is to highlight textual complexity, not to straighten it out."[4]

For the sake of holding textual complexity, it is helpful to account for how literary criticisms (note the plural) entered the theater of biblical studies. While literary criticism emerged in biblical studies in the 1970s when biblical scholars began to adopt and adapt secular literary criticism in more formal ways,[5] "literary criticisms and theories span over 2,500 years of time and space."[6] Nothing of what surfaces in the field of biblical interpretation happens in a bubble. Biblical scholars do not just make stuff up; that which gets infused into the discipline reflects surrounding trends. In the case of literary theory, when postmodernism in the 1960s and 1970s questioned the "metanarratives" assumed by modernism, the historical-critical method that had reigned in biblical scholarship since its formal inception also fell under scrutiny. This "so-called literary paradigm shift" hinged on the distinction between "diachronic" and "synchronic" approaches to the interpretation of texts: diachronic analyses focusing on the "biblical texts as they've developed over time" and synchronic analyses "looking at a text as it is at a single moment in time."[7] It is this focus on synchronic literary approaches that moves biblical criticism along a trajectory of new questions and varied approaches based on the Bible as literature.

Of course, how to classify literature and literary theory becomes critical. Dinkler defines literature as "written poetry or prose that communicates through the use of specific linguistic techniques, and that is taken by society to be meaningful beyond its immediate context of origin." Correspondingly, then, literary theory "investigates the means by which humans make meaning through written poetry and prose."[8]

For biblical scholars, this embrace of various aspects of secular literary theory morphed into what became "narrative criticism," investigating features of biblical narratives namely narrator, point of view, time, plot, characters, and rhetorical features such as irony.[9] "Narrative criticism is a development within biblical scholarship which, though initially based on the theoretical studies of non-biblical literary critics . . . , has incorporated a variety of insights from these critics which have evolved into an eclectic form of literary criticism with no direct counterpart in non-biblical literary criticism."[10] In the end, a literary approach to biblical interpretation "offers the promise that, just as we all enjoy a good story, play, or film, we might also delight in the experience of reading the Bible."[11]

SUMMARY OF THE APPROACH

Without a taxonomy for literary approaches, navigating the field is unwieldy at best. For this discussion, therefore, we will lean on Dinkler's use of a scheme offered by Meyer Abrams, a diagrammatic structure "organized around four poles of interpretive polarization: An *author* composes a *text* for a *reader* about the *universe*."[12] Within these identifying poles, however, there is not a balance of attention, because "every critical approach to literature leans more heavily toward one orientation or another."[13] Having this taxonomy in mind is also essential when engaging any kind of theoretical perspective. That is, "theory, in all of its iterations, pushes us to recognize, first, the *power of normativity*, and second, the *necessity of critical reflexivity*."[14]

Dinkler describes four interpretive poles:

Mimetic, universe-oriented approach. From this pole, "the literary text imitates the world it portrays." It is looking for "what a text reports about its world."[15]

Expressive, author-oriented approach. These "expressive forms of criticism locate the meaning of a literary text in the message that its author intended to convey."[16] Phrases such as "authorial intent" are connected with this approach. In the world of biblical interpretation, scholars who focus on this approach examine the literary features of a text to "discern its ancient author's (or final redactor's) original intentions."[17] Under this label appears rhetorical criticism, with which scholars try to achieve a better understanding of the movement of the author's thought, intent, and message.[18] Examining an author's use of and purpose for specific rhetorical devices, such as irony, for example, would also fall under this category.

Work-oriented, objective approach. These approaches "deal with the literary text as an object of study in its own right." To be clear, they are not called "objective" because they are "without presupposition or bias, but because they consider the meaning of a work to be independent of its relation to reality, independent of its author's intent, and independent of its audience's responses."[19] In biblical interpretation, scholars who follow this approach have adopted the "literary subfield of narratology" to develop "narrative criticism."[20]

Pragmatic, audience-oriented approach. This approach has as its "main focus the literary text's effects upon its audience/s." In classical rhetoric, this approach can also represent the art of persuasion, though not every rhetorical piece intends to be suasive. Biblical critics who have adopted this approach often describe their work as "reader-response" criticism. There is, therefore, "greater emphasis on the audience's constitutive role in meaning-making as a social construction."[21]

As helpful as this taxonomy is for organizing the vast array of literary approaches appropriated by biblical scholarship, the astute reader quickly realizes the false assurances of categorization. Overlap is inevitable. But at the very least, we have a way forward that might demonstrate how "the tools provided for interpretation presume the type of interpretation that should be produced." Another access point into the world of literary theory and the Bible is to remember that literary theory tends to three "sets of issues: hermeneutical matters (how language functions, where textual meaning resides); evaluative concerns (how we assess the literary value of a text); metadisciplinary views (what critics ought to be reading and doing vis-à-vis the literary)."[22]

Out of the intersection of literary approaches and cultural sensitivities, that is, the pragmatic, audience-oriented approach, is born the approaches that are reviewed in the remaining chapters of this book. For the sake of clarity, but trying not to border on tedium, below are three literary paradigms that preachers might employ in their sermon preparation. Having the capacity to identify these approaches helps in our readerly expectations. Don't ask a commentator to tell you what that commentator is not interested in giving you.

Using the four-pole taxonomy as guide, the first paradigm is the *formalist literary paradigm*, which "focuses on the autonomous literary form of the text as it stands."[23] These approaches fall under work-oriented, objective approaches. Under this rubric, meaning cannot be determined apart from the form. The form is not a benign feature of the text. To distinguish even further, in biblical studies, "form critics are interested in the *earliest forms* of the NT texts and tradition, while literary formalists focus on a text's *extant form* (from any given point in time)."[24] We might make the comparison to taking into consideration the form that is a parable or the form that is an existing overall narrative.

The second literary paradigm is *structuralism*, "which assumes that universal principles structure human communication." Put another way, meaning is found in the "invisible design of language itself . . . with the universal codes and conventions that make such a work possible."[25] Under this paradigm exist studies such as narratology, genre theory, Marxism, Neo-Marxism, psychoanalysis, and even feminism. The overall point of structuralist interest is "the hermeneutical conviction that texts function according to universal deep structures."[26] An interpretive task within this paradigm is to describe the structures at work in a text that are determinative of meaning.

A third literary paradigm is what Dinkler describes as *poststructuralism and beyond*. The definition that one might ascribe to poststructuralism is likely correct on the first guess—the rejection of "stable underlying structures of language" and any claims of "totality and universality."[27] By embracing particularism, poststructuralism calls into question the underpinnings of language as a priori. "Poststructuralists stress that because humans perceive the world from our own partial and particular points of view, our perceptions of reality necessarily change according to shifts in time, location, and culture. People make sense and draw connections—that is to say, people *mean*—differently."[28] Born out of this belief came "a 'new species' of literary criticism" recognized as "identity-based approaches,"[29] which include third-wave feminism, womanism, gender studies, queer theory, and the circumstances of race, ethnicity, cultures, territories, and nations in literature (postcolonial criticism falls under this category). Postcolonial approaches, specifically as they focus on particular ethnicities and cultures, include African American, Native American, Asian, and Latinx criticisms.

Poststructuralism and beyond has been the cause of great consternation and resistance, particularly within the field of biblical interpretation. Critics claim that this is reading the Bible with an "agenda" or leads one down the slippery slope of relativism. The point is, of course, that all reading, all meaning making, is subjectively determined. While complex, "literary matters are at the heart of NT interpretation." Literary theory is a "labyrinthine land"[30] but a necessary adventure for anyone who wishes to make public interpretations of biblical texts. And an adventure it is, inviting us to "savor the pleasure of literature well written," allowing and pondering the gaps in the story, setting aside our insistences on "what really happened," and expecting to "experience irony, suspense, and surprise."[31]

Where does this leave us? Identity-based approaches within literary criticism will have their individual chapters below as each asks its own specific questions that demand our nuanced attention. For the rest of this chapter, the focus will be on literary interpretation that represents the work-oriented, objective approach, with an eye toward the formalist literary paradigm.

A balcony view might serve as an apt conclusion to this section:

> Biblical literature embodies the cultural moment in which it arises. In this, it's like all literature—looking ahead to new possibility and looking back to lessons from the past. Literature can challenge the presumptions of our predecessors, pushing us to imagine new possibilities and inspiring us to pursue new ways of being. And literature can uphold the status quo, authorizing us to cling to our biases and look away from injustice.[32]

Preachers might well ask themselves, then, How will I define biblical literature? What do I want this literature to be, to do? Honest answers to those questions move us further toward ethical preaching.

SAMPLE TEXT: JOHN 13–17

With all that has been stated above, bringing a literary approach, or approaches, to a passage in John could result in an entire book. Selectivity is essential, along with a substantive dose of reflexivity. Because the majority of this book is dedicated to the second and third paradigms, structuralism and poststructuralism and beyond, the analysis in this chapter will focus on the first one, the formalist literary paradigm.

Another way to identify this approach is Mark Allan Powell's "ordering of events" and "duration and frequency of events" in narrative analysis. "The order in which a narrative relates events is important because readers are expected to consider each new episode in light of what has gone before." As for duration and frequency, "Reader's perceptions concerning the events of a narrative may be influenced by the amount of space given to reporting individual episodes or by the number of times that a particular event is referenced in the narrative."[33]

The sample text for this exercise is the Farewell Discourse in the Gospel of John (John 13–17).[34] The literary form or genre of the discourse itself is important to note up front. Jesus' final words to his disciples have been compared to other farewell addresses in ancient literature, from both Jewish and Greco-Roman sources. In the Old Testament, farewell words are offered by Jacob (Gen. 49), Joseph (Gen. 50), Moses (Deut. 31–32), Joshua (Josh. 24), and David (1 Chr. 29). In the New Testament, Acts 20 presents Paul's farewell.

Scholars set out differing parameters for the Farewell Discourse, depending on whether they include the footwashing in John 13. It is tempting to begin the discourse at 14:1, the convenient chapter demarcation, yet as chapters, verses, paragraphing, and punctuation did not exist in the original manuscripts of the New Testament, one could argue for the start of the discourse at 13:31, where, after Judas's departure, Jesus begins to interpret the "sign" he just performed with and for his disciples, that is, the footwashing, and the signs that are yet to come (the crucifixion and resurrection).

Regardless of specific verse decisions, the length and location of the Farewell Discourse in John is worth discussion. While chapters 1–12 (often titled the Book of Signs) span the three-year ministry of Jesus, chapters 13–21 narrate the events of roughly one week, with chapters 13–17 given over to one night. A narrative block of five chapters devoted to the last night Jesus has with his disciples reinforces the poignancy of the moment. The narrative space dedicated to Jesus' last words and last hours with his disciples demands an interpretive approach that mimics the elongation of time. We cannot rush through these chapters for the sake of an interpretive end. Rather, the length of Jesus' final address almost halts time; it invites readers to hang on Jesus' every word, just as his disciples needed to. The Farewell Discourse is an interruption of the narrative flow, the plot, of the Gospel. We are forced to stop and to take seriously the effect of this interruption on the meaning of the words themselves.

The Farewell Discourse, Jesus' final words to his disciples before his arrest in John 18, is unique to John's Gospel. Many of the Gospel's themes find expression in the discourse, and, in that regard, the discourse serves as Jesus' interpretation of his entire ministry. A literary-critical approach might elicit a vast number of hermeneutical possibilities, but this analysis will be limited to one example of how the narratology of a text communicates meaning. Or, to say it differently, how "the narrative mode makes a theological claim."[35] Specifically, we will look at the structure and occurrence of the Paraclete passages in the Farewell Discourse and what this formal structure communicates for the interpretation of the role of the Paraclete in the Fourth Gospel.

While there have been references to the Spirit in the narrative up to this point (1:32–33; 3:5, 6, 8, 34; 4:23, 24; 6:63; 7:39; 11:33), the focused exposition of John's pneumatology is located in the Farewell Discourse. For the first time, the Holy Spirit is identified as Paraclete (*paraklētos*). This compound word made up of *para* (alongside) and *klētos*, from the verb *kaleō* (to call), denotes the spirit as "the one who is called alongside." This distinctive pneumatological image is translated numerous ways—advocate, comforter, companion, counselor, helper, aide, guide—in contemporary English translations of the New Testament. Interpretation of the Paraclete and John's pneumatology from a literary approach must consider why the introduction and development of the Holy Spirit as Paraclete occurs here in the narrative.

With such a consideration in mind, we note how and where the Paraclete is present. In response to the troubling spirit of the moment, Jesus says, "And I will ask the Father, and he will give you another Advocate, to be with you forever" (14:16). Before Jesus' promise of the gift of the Paraclete, Judas has betrayed Jesus by exiting the room: "Immediately he went out. And it was night" (13:30). Judas's abandonment of his relationship with Jesus—and his relationship with his fellow disciples—has been the subject of the conversation thus far. After the footwashing, Jesus predicts Judas's departure. "After saying this

Jesus was troubled in spirit, and declared, 'Very truly, I tell you, one of you will betray me'" (v. 21). The disciples look around at each other, wondering, Who could it be? The abandonment by Judas is contrasted with the abiding of the disciple whom Jesus loves, first introduced into the narrative in 13:23: "One of his disciples—the one whom Jesus loved—was reclining next to him." Immediately on the heels of Judas's betrayal is Jesus' command to love one another (vv. 31–35), which also contains Jesus' announcement that he is leaving: "Little children, I am with you only a little longer. You will look for me; and as I said to the Jews so now I say to you, 'Where I am going, you cannot come'" (v. 33). This is followed by yet another cause for troubled hearts, the foretelling of Peter's denial (vv. 36–38). It is into these multiple losses that Jesus gives the promise of the Paraclete, the one who will accompany the disciples in Jesus' absence. Any understanding of the role of the Paraclete and John's pneumatology demands careful attention to this literary context. The Paraclete will have a very specific purpose because of the narrative space in which the Paraclete is introduced.

A formalist literary approach also observes that the discussion of the Holy Spirit occurs in three distinct locations in the Farewell Discourse. The first has been discussed above (14:15–17, 25–26). The second presentation of the Paraclete is in chapter 15 (vv. 26–27) and the third in chapter 16 (vv. 4b–15). With these three separate locations spread out over the course of Jesus' farewell words, the Paraclete, the one who is called to be alongside the disciples, literarily accompanies them. Positioning Jesus' promise of the Paraclete in each chapter of the Farewell Discourse underscores the purpose and identity of the Paraclete as accompanier, as companion. The narrative mode, the form that the pneumatological discourse takes on, reinforces the theological claim.

Once this formal structure is determined, the surrounding narrative takes on new meaning as well. Each pneumatological discourse follows moments of deep distress for the disciples and for Jesus. The first introduction of the Paraclete succeeds the betrayal of Judas, the foreshadowing of Peter's denial, Jesus' initial intimations of his departure, and Thomas's desperate plea, "Lord, we do not know where you are going. How can we know the way?" (14:5). In chapter 15, the promise of the Paraclete ensues from Jesus' words about the world's hatred and impending persecution of both Jesus and his disciples (vv. 18–24). The third pneumatological discourse follows the third reference in the Fourth Gospel to being "put out of the synagogue" (16:2). In chapter 9, this is the fear of the parents of the man born blind. "His parents said this because they were afraid of the Jews; for the Jews had already agreed that anyone who confessed Jesus to be the Messiah would be put out of the synagogue. Therefore his parents said, 'He is of age; ask him'" (9:22–23). Their concern reflects that of the Johannine community, followers of Jesus, believing him to be the Messiah, who were likely cast out of their synagogue for this confession.[36] Each promise of the presence and activity of the Paraclete arises from the most troubling words of Jesus about his future and the future of the disciples. The narrative locations of the promise of the Paraclete give emphasis to John's unique pneumatology, a pneumatology that understands the Holy Spirit as the companion to the faithful, who will accompany believers in what lies ahead.

HOMILETICAL IMPLICATIONS

Reading the Bible as literature is compelling. There is an inherent allure when it comes to literary approaches and the interpretation of the Bible. Who doesn't love a good story? Furthermore, "Literary interpretation promises to make the Bible more accessible to non-specialists."[37] A sermon is neither an exegetical paper nor a report on the preacher's prowess, but is, in part, an invitation into a storied world filled with a variety of characters, plot twists and turns, intriguing settings, captivating details, and narrative flourish. When the preacher tends the literary features of a biblical text, already the passage will take on a kind of appeal as Scripture becomes something more than a dictionary for faith or a book of rules. The Gospel writers are, all of a sudden, messengers of truth as "imaginative, creative crafters of art."[38]

A literary approach is a source of empowerment for the listener. As noted in the introduction, the advent of literary interpretation of the Bible also brought attention to the response of the reader, with the idea that the text does not hold an inherent and unchangeable meaning, but meaning happens between text and reader. The reader is not a passive recipient of information but an active agent in meaning making. At the same time, textual instability may be a frightening prospect for many in our pews. When the dominant Christian voices posit textual inerrancy and readerly objectivity, suggesting that readers have an interpretive role beyond, or in place of, discovering the text's nugget of gospel truth could very well lead to opposition and rejection. Negotiating this terrain will necessitate some pastoral sensitivity. We have a long way to go toward egalitarian interpretation of the Bible.

Pointing out narrative features in a biblical text suggests to the hearers that they can do the same. A seminary degree is not a prerequisite for interpreting the Bible. People can approach Scripture with the same curiosity and anticipation as they would a novel, even venturing meaning as they would for their favorite genre of literature. Geographical notations become places of and for meaning—what is Jesus doing in Sychar, of all places? Did he really have to go through Samaria to get to Galilee from Jerusalem (4:1–6)? Biblical people become subjects of characterization. What do we make of Nicodemus and his role in the story (3:1–21; 7:45–52; 19:38–42)? Differences in plot are cause for investigation—why is the temple incident in chapter 2 of John and not at the end of Jesus' public ministry, as in the Synoptic Gospels? A narrative detail stops the flow of reading and pulls us up short—why did the woman leave her water jar behind at the well (4:28)? Appreciation for the literary artistry of the biblical writers might lead to a different kind of engagement with the Bible, one that is more dialogical, like sitting down over a cup of coffee with a good conversation partner.

At the same time, an egalitarian hermeneutic also means that preachers will have to give up control of the narrative. This requires coming to terms with one's own assumed or hoped-for meanings in texts and acknowledging one's own understanding of the authority of Scripture and one's theological biases. Such self-reflection is rarely altogether pleasant, but it is necessary for homiletical honesty. And yet, letting go of control is precisely what happens anyway, regardless of our best efforts to keep things in check. We know instinctively that listeners hear what they need or want to hear and then eagerly share what they heard, which is rarely what the speaker intended.

Literary approaches can also be a fount of encouragement for the preacher who longs for wonder when it comes to interpreting the Bible. So often preoccupied by the search for the meaning of a text that will yield a sermon, preachers set aside imagination for results. Interpreting the Bible as literature might spark renewed enthusiasm for engaging Scripture, perhaps even a reorientation of the preacher's relationship with God's Word. Allowing ourselves to be caught up in our curiosities also slows down our reading. Pushing to the end of a pericope will not necessarily yield a sermon focus. Meaning can be found in the smallest of details, which are often overlooked in our quest for a homiletical point or our assumption that a sermon must cover the entirety of the biblical passage set before us. At the same time, a literary sensitivity is not sought for the sake of itself but for what it generates theologically.

The goal is not pointing out a narrative detail, but realizing how that narrative detail reinforces or gives meaning to a theological claim.

The Farewell Discourse as a genre, as Jesus' final words to his disciples, sets out thematic and interpretive expectations for meaning and preaching. The purpose and tone of Jesus' last speech to his followers should determine the same for the sermon. That is, a sermon on the Farewell Discourse should imitate the genre's intent and mood. When a sermon lacks this kind of biblical alignment, the text's homiletical potential is not fully reached. One might even ask if a sermon is biblical if it does not pay attention to the "how" of the text and not just the "what." Noting the formal structure of the pneumatological discourses within the Farewell Discourse affirms the pneumatology of John as a whole. The Fourth Evangelist offers a unique understanding of the person and role of the Holy Spirit as the one who will accompany the disciples in Jesus' absence. A preacher might feel encouraged to preach the specificity of John's pneumatology when the narrative mode is recognized as supporting the theological claim. In this regard, the preacher is faithful to John's pneumatology when the pull toward harmonization is ever more potent if a doctrine of the church is at stake, especially on a day like Pentecost.

In a related manner, attention to the literary and narrative components of biblical texts is a counteraction to the dominant experience of the Bible in our churches—pericopes dislodged from their narrative homes. Resituating a passage into its literary context has the potential to address biblical illiteracy, to correct misinterpretations when texts are removed from their contexts, and to prod new interpretive possibilities when connections are made between the part and the whole, between the whole and the part. When "the Bible says" is common parlance, it is the preacher's responsibility to respond, "But where, why, when, to whom, and for what purpose?" What hermeneutical and homiletical possibilities have been shortchanged because a passage has been wrenched from its literary context? It is part of our calling to help listeners to be better readers of the Bible, which demands dogged faithfulness, responsibility, and accountability.

Another homiletical observation when it comes to literary approaches and biblical interpretation is to notice how the interpretive polarization taxonomy presented in the "Summary of the Approach" section mirrors what the preacher might know as the Rhetorical Triangle. As a form of rhetoric, homiletics moves about the Rhetorical Triangle. The homiletical project is a constant conversation between the text, or logos (mimetic/objective); the community/audience, or pathos (pragmatic); and the preacher/speaker, the ethos or artist (expressive). While literary critics of the Bible might have the luxury to choose on which pole to stake an argument, the preacher is not as fortunate. A sermon falls flat or does not "fit" when one of these angles is left out of our inherited homiletical geometry. In homiletical terms, preachers constantly have in mind their own character (preacher/speaker/ethos/artist) and what will be revealed about, what is at stake for, their character in the sermon. Preachers read the biblical text and engage the world through the eyes and ears and hearts of their congregations or ministry communities (community/audience/pathos). The sermon is always for a particular place and people, and not for general consumption. Preachers are charged with a specific object for or of the sermon as a rhetorical event, and that object/subject matter/material is the Word (mimetic/object/ logos). The subject matter for a sermon, however, is not an object but a person, the revelation of God in Jesus, the Word made flesh, which distinguishes a sermon from a speech.

Literary approaches warrant some homiletical cautions. These concerns are not meant to scare the preacher off from this appealing approach, but to call attention to the ways in which we preachers are beholden to a kind of normativity for Scripture that is caught up in the holy. That is, the Bible is not just or simply literature, but is communication of, from, and about the Divine. The preacher, the interpreter, navigates a fine line between aesthetic expectations and theological meaning. Even our leanings toward certain translations betray an assumption of the pleasingness of Scripture because of what it communicates—a divine presence. Testifying to the holy should be beautiful. At the same time, layers of denominational demography, ecclesial history, and ideological systems often hold sway, preventing us from believing that theological meaning can happen outside of concrete confessional and creedal claims. This means that we must name the expectations we have of biblical texts that might cause us to bracket them off from analytical or theoretical methods, a reminder appropriate for all approaches set forth in this book.

FURTHER RESOURCES FOR PREACHING

Graves, Mike, and David Schlafer, eds. *What's the Shape of Narrative Preaching?* St. Louis: Chalice Press, 2008.

2

Postcolonial Biblical Interpretation

INTRODUCTION

Postcolonial interpretation first acknowledges and names the sordid history of colonialism in our world, examining "the impact created by Western colonization on individuals, communities, and cultures."[1] This means that postcolonial criticism is a reckoning with our colonial past as deeply shaping communal and individual identity in the present.

Colonialism "refers to the settlement and/or exploitation of a territory by foreign agents,"[2] and in particular, "the domination of third world peoples by the West."[3] In this regard, "empires came to exist because particular nations or groups determined that they had a right or responsibility to attain the resources of others and to control foreign populations."[4] Although colonial empires began to break apart after World War II, as third-world countries sought freedom from occupation, this does not mean that colonialism disappeared. In fact, "the contemporary world exists as it does because of colonial/imperial history"[5] and will continue to do so. Colonialism is not limited by territorialism, that is, easily delineated boundaries or regions being infiltrated, but can be detected in behaviors and tactics in which empire asserts domination. In other words, colonialism is not simply that which demarcates a colonized territory but remains in existence because of its driving philosophical force: "Imperialism is the ideology from which colonialism arises."[6]

We exist in a world where "we are living the consequences of colonial history and encountering colonialism in contemporary guises."[7] To engage in postcolonial criticism is to acknowledge that even though there have been successes in independences from colonizing controls, the heritages of colonization and its ideological framework remain.

In the field of criticisms, "postcolonial studies emerged as a way of engaging with the textual, historical, and cultural articulations of societies disturbed and transformed by the historical reality of colonial presence." This means that "*postcolonial* does not suggest that empire and colonialism/imperialism are safely located in the past, but suggests that we continue to be affected by them." Or, put another way, "Our lives are played out on the stage of empire. While *colonizing discourse* may not be a familiar term for most, it is a familiar discourse. We are accustomed to a world in which some dominate, in which some people should be kept apart from others, in which homogeneity is valued over diversity, in which there is a preference for one, single worldview."[8]

The term "postcolonial" has composite connotations. In chronological terms, "postcolonial" represents the time after the 1960s and the downfall of modern European imperialism. (Postcolonial analysis distinguishes between imperialism and colonialism: imperialism refers to "whatever has to do with the dominant centre," and colonialism points "to whatever has to do with the subordinated periphery."[9]) Frequently, this historical period, as the aftermath of being colonized persons, is designated as "post-colonial" with the hyphen intact. In this regard, "post-colonial" can also be viewed as the condition of no longer being a colony, and "as finding a space in the world as a newly independent nation state." At the same time, "postcolonial" without the hyphen has been understood as "resistance discourse"[10] whereby the formerly colonized criticize dominant systems that perpetuate their own normativity, "in order to recover the past from the Western slander and misinformation of the colonial period."[11] Postcolonialism as resistance discourse also questions "neo-colonizing tendencies"[12] even after the securing of independence.

In this regard, "postcolonial" can be understood as "the ongoing reality of those whose social histories have been shaped and continue to be shaped culturally, psychologically, and economically by the reality of colonialism/imperialism and the concomitant interplay of power related to gender, race, and class."[13] Postcolonial criticism is then birthed by the testimony of colonized people and, at the same time, is vigilant in its interrogation of how political and social power is exerted over others.

As such, postcolonialism concerns itself with imbalances of power and the "social, cultural, political, and historical contexts in which domestication takes place."[14] It is a stance of inquiry, a set of critical possibilities or articulated aptitudes, with the primary focus being to disclose the inner workings of powers to dominate and deny rights, to subjugate and control.

SUMMARY OF THE APPROACH

Like other critical movements, postcolonial criticism finds its way into biblical interpretation via adoption and adaptation of the perceived secular approach for and into biblical studies, focusing "on the relationship between literature . . . and imperialism."[15] At the same time, it is an avenue of interpretation that finds resonance in the biblical writings as witnesses to active colonization and communities being colonized. Postcolonial biblical interpretation became a field of investigation following the essential premises of postcolonial literary criticism in the mid-1990s. "Postcolonial studies emerged as a way of engaging with the textual, historical, and cultural articulations of societies disturbed and transformed by the historical reality of colonial presence, arriving in the nineteen-eighties along with other kinds of resistance literature/theories."[16]

As noted above, postcolonial interpretation is a vast and compound collection of approaches that defies easy categorization, in part because it reflects the complexity of world colonialism and localized situations. "Postcolonialism was never conceived as a grand theory, but as creative literature and as a resistance discourse emerging in the former colonies of the Western empires."[17] Or, as Warren Carter describes it, "This cluster of theories, this different way of seeing, this optic, places non-Western interests first and resists any attempt to view them as inferior to Western interests. It opposes oppressive power. It looks from below."[18] This recognition of perspective is especially critical for biblical studies, in which Western interpretation has dominated the scholarly landscape.

As postcolonialism puts in view imperial domination and domestication in social, cultural, political, and historical spheres, its role in and for biblical narratives becomes invaluable. The examination of how power and politics serve as thematic material in biblical literature becomes front and center. A postcolonial perspective that has an eye to constructions of and challenges to power and politics is essential for a collection of books in which claims for power dominate the narratives. A postcolonial approach focuses on how "expansion, domination, and imperialism" shape "both the biblical narratives and biblical interpretation."[19] Empire, imperialism, and colonialism are inescapable realities of the world of antiquity and our modern world. Postcolonialism ferrets out these truths of societal structures and exposes their inherent oppression of the other. "A postcolonial perspective denotes a desire to recognize and interrupt colonizing discourses and to uncover embedded colonial/imperial assumptions that guide daily life." Furthermore, "postcolonial biblical interpretation considers the manner in which the Bible has been implicated in the colonial/imperial process, and also how it speaks a word of liberation into a postcolonial ethos." The Bible and its interpretation cannot be exempt from the imperialism in the history of civilization, because "biblical texts have been co-opted as partners in colonial/imperial projects and can potentially serve to justify imperial projects or even colonizing discourse."[20]

In the case of biblical interpretation, postcolonialism also names the hegemony of Western thought in biblical criticism, or, how "the shadow of empire in the production of modern readings of the ancient texts"[21] still has a large cast. In other words, postcolonial criticism is an active form of investigation when it comes to biblical interpretation; at the same time, it intentionally exposes the ways in which imperial Western Christianity has dominated biblical interpretation. It is, if you will, a criticism of historical criticism.

In addition, postcolonialism offers a view into the New Testament writings that can give voice to the reality of Palestine as a Roman colony. Colonial Palestine is the subtext of the writings of the New Testament. The assertion of Jesus' power and authority is not only or simply a theological claim but also a proposal for Jesus' absolute power and authority over and against imperial Rome. Jesus is crucified under Roman rule and law, sentenced to death by the Roman governor, Pontius Pilate. A postcolonial perspective erases "the delusion that NT texts are neutral or apolitical (a-imperial) or solely 'spiritual.'"[22]

At the same time, and especially in the four Gospels, we see Jesus in conflict with the local rulers of colonial Palestine, the religious leaders such as the Pharisees, Sadducees, and Herodians. Postcolonial criticism enables reflection on these conflicts without going down the road of anti-Semitism. These clashes were not about decrying Judaism and its religious structures—Jesus, of course, was a Jew. They are, rather, a critique from the wider perspective of colonizing principles. As religion is one aspect of political life and an arm of control, in postcolonial interpretation, the regional institutions and authorities are also placed under the microscope for their propensity toward power over and exploitation of the other. Warren Carter summarizes this issue: "The Gospels, then, are understood to be representations that oppose as well as assume and encode imperial dynamics as part of their various strategies of negotiation. The Gospels emerge as writings from relatively powerless groups that are both somewhat accommodated to imperial structures as a basic form of survival, yet are also committed to a different understanding of the world and its transformation according to God's purposes (or empire!)."[23]

SAMPLE TEXT: JOHN 3:1–21

The Gospel of John has had a significant role in postcolonial critical studies. This prominence is due, in part, to the Fourth Gospel's forthright expression of the absolute power and authority of Jesus over all authoritative counterparts. The Fourth Gospel is a macro-political project, concerned with contexts of "the local and 'national,' by way of regional conflict among various groupings with the area of colonial Palestine; the global or 'international,' in terms of the Roman Empire; the cosmic or 'transworldly,' through mythical conflict between suprahuman powers with the conception of reality as a whole."[24] The thoroughness with which the Fourth Evangelist seeks to dismantle and disrupt all "dominions and allegiances" leads Segovia, for example, to identify John as a "postcolonial proposal."[25] In the wide-reaching conflict narrated by John, no element of life, and thus no person, is without judgment if it attempts to wield power that is antithetical to God's abiding love. This conflict occurs "at the cosmic level, between God, sovereign of the world above, and Satan, sovereign of the world below—at the global level, between Jesus, Word of God and Saviour of the world, and the imperial rulers of Rome—at the local level, between Jesus, Word of God and Messiah of the Jews, and the colonial elite of Judaea."[26]

Bringing a postcolonial perspective to bear on the encounter between Jesus and Nicodemus in John 3:1–21 yields a number of insights for the interpretation and preaching of a passage that is consistently overtheologized, especially in favor of developed Christianity and the holy catholic church as institution.[27] For example, interpreters and preachers frequently understand Jesus' words to Nicodemus, "Very truly, I tell you, no one can enter the kingdom of God without being born of water and Spirit" (John 3:5), as an allusion to the rite of baptism, even though baptism and even Jesus' baptism are significantly downplayed in the Gospel of John as a means of professing belief and community membership.[28] Whereas in the Synoptic Gospels Jesus' baptism and his temptation in the wilderness are the events that incentivize Jesus' public ministry, in John the encouragement comes from his mother at the wedding at Cana (2:1–11). Jesus' baptism in John functions to confirm Jesus' identity, to which John the Baptist testifies, and there is no temptation in the wilderness in the Fourth Gospel.

Through a postcolonial perspective, even before reading the encounter between Jesus and Nicodemus, the setting and narrative location of the conversation point immediately to the presence and realities of the conflict of powers. Jesus is in Jerusalem, the religious center of Judaism, and not in Galilee. Jesus is in Jerusalem for Passover (2:13), unlike the Synoptic Gospels, which have Jesus in Jerusalem only once—at the end of his ministry, just before his arrest, trial, crucifixion, and death. The setting alone, therefore, from a postcolonial lens, calls attention to and highlights a clashing of authorities and powers.

Exacerbating this conflict of authority is the relocation of the temple incident in John to chapter 2, a divergent move from the chronology presented in Matthew, Mark, and Luke. There are several reasons for and interpretations of the alternative setting for this event. Most salient from a postcolonial perspective, however, is that the relocation of the temple incident brings the opposition between Jesus and the religious authorities to the forefront of the narrative. The temple incident is the second public act of Jesus' ministry, immediately after the wedding at Cana. These juxtaposed events underscore the potential of Jesus' authority and power.

The details recorded in John's version of the temple incident are also important from a postcolonial viewpoint. Jesus does not say, "You have made [my Father's house] a den of robbers," as he does in Matthew 21:13, Mark 11:17, and Luke 19:46, but "Stop making my Father's house a marketplace" (John 2:16). The historical and religious reality was, however, that the temple had to be a marketplace for the temple system to continue to exist. Offerings, such as grains, especially for the three pilgrimage festivals (Passover, Weeks, and Booths), would be brought by observant Jews from as far away as the Galilean region to exchange for the required animal sacrifices for the festivals. A challenge to the foundation of the religious sacrificial system would have had rippling ramifications—not just religious, but historical, political, and cultural. Jesus then defies the authorities, "Destroy this temple, and in three days I will raise it up" (2:19). The authorities respond, "This temple has been under construction for forty-six years, and will you raise it up in three days?" (v. 20). This exchange heightens the conflict even more. Not only is this a threat to the Jewish religious system, but it is also a threat to their standing and survival as a colonized people. Of course, John was written after the razing of Jerusalem and destruction of the temple, but that historical event was a result of general unrest and then the Jewish revolt of 66–70 CE. The empire strikes back, even more a present and potent reality with the relocation in John of the temple incident.

The theological reason for moving the temple incident in John is to underscore the presence of God in the incarnated Jesus—not in the temple—"but he was speaking of the temple of his body" (v. 21). John's Christology and theology demand the new setting in the narrative. The dismantling of the temple and its sacrificial system, however, is not a rejection of Judaism but upholding Jesus as the Word made flesh, the I AM. At the same time, it challenges a power system unable to recognize God's way of love in Jesus and calls attention to a colonial mind-set of survival.

Jesus' presence in Jerusalem, so early in the Gospel, and the temple incident thus serve as the backdrop for the encounter between Jesus and Nicodemus. Given this setting and Nicodemus's role as a representative of the Jewish authorities with whom Jesus has already collided, there is very little reason to view Nick at night in a positive light. We might want to give him the benefit of the doubt, lending him a sympathetic ear, but the immediate surroundings make that difficult to justify. Nicodemus holds power and authority that are just as much in question as Roman power and authority. Bringing a postcolonial lens to the characterization of Nicodemus may meet some resistance. We want to save Nicodemus. We want to find in him hope for any person, regardless of their lot in life, to see in Jesus God's power and presence. If, as Segovia argues, John as a postcolonial project allows no authoritative group to escape scrutiny, then there really is only one outcome for

Nicodemus, whose loyalties are lodged with his religious structures and not with a movement that jeopardizes his standing, as precarious as it is amid Roman rule and reign.

When we realize our own inclinations to rescue Nicodemus or when we find ourselves wanting to confirm our confidence in his earnestness, to admire his risk taking, or to take to heart his genuine searching, postcolonialism turns the table on the interpreter. We want to justify Nicodemus because our own desire for power is on the line. We want to affirm that his motives are legitimate and earnest because we want ours to be as well. Taking seriously the kind of power Nicodemus has and the power he likely wants to keep demands that we ask ourselves, Just what empire are we serving? What status quo are we trying to maintain? What authoritative systems preclude us from recognizing God's power? What dominant center are we protecting? How do our institutions continue to control and oppress? Who are we trying to assimilate for the sake of homogeneity?

As noted above, sermons frequently hyperspiritualize the story of Nicodemus, making specific connections to baptism. "Being born of water and Spirit" must be a reference to baptism, when within the narrative as a whole, statements about water and Spirit are not directly connected to baptism and invite larger connotations. John the Baptist notes that he himself baptizes with water (1:26, 31, 33) and testifies as he witnesses the baptism of Jesus, "I myself did not know him, but the one who sent me to baptize with water said to me, 'He on whom you see the Spirit descend and remain is the one who baptizes with the Holy Spirit'" (v. 33), but other references to baptism do not correlate the Spirit with the kind of baptizing that Jesus is doing (3:22, 26; 4:1–2). While there is nothing inherently wrong with interpreting Scripture through a sacramental lens, this move is often limited and determined by our own denominational loyalties and commitments, which historically exclude.

The use of baptism in colonization meant that Christian missionaries held power of and over salvation. Baptism became the rite for church membership and ultimately salvation. One might ask, for example, how a Native American would respond to an interpretation of "unless you are born of water and Spirit" as a baptismal image and mandate, given the North American history of mass conversion and assimilation of indigenous persons. Postcolonialism forces reflection on hegemonic attitudes about sacramental practices. And while we are keen on inserting our baptismal beliefs and practices into the passage, we are less eager to allow the passage itself to shape or interpret our contemporary baptismal beliefs and practices.

When "born again/anew/from above" is heard from a postcolonial perspective, alternative interpretive possibilities come into view. "Born" is used eight times in John 3:3–8, after the first occurrence of *gennaō* in John 1:12–13, "But to all who received him, who believed in his name, he gave power to become children of God, who were born, not of blood or of the will of the flesh or of the will of man, but of God." While Nicodemus takes Jesus' words literally, in the larger context of the Johannine narrative, "children of God" communicates primarily relationship—with God and with Jesus—and, more specifically, intimates a dependence on God. Nicodemus's focus on the literal level indicates not only his inability to understand Jesus' offering but also his unwillingness to accept it. In Nicodemus's response is, then, incredulity based on assumptions he holds from his religious system. To be born again/anew/from above is a statement about allegiances, not necessarily a spiritualized affiliation.

Jesus is inviting Nicodemus into a dependent relationship, one that is not theoretical, but embracing the identity of being a child of God. Children in the ancient world had no power. If Nicodemus accepts Jesus' offer, he gives up power and authority. His status plummets to the bottom of the hierarchical social systems of the first century. No wonder Nicodemus responds, "How can these things be?" Nicodemus's incredulity might not be a misunderstanding of rebirth or being born again/anew/from above, but a rejection of what Jesus is requesting of him. We want to assume that "how can these things be?" communicates an inability of Nicodemus to wrap his head around what Jesus is saying and what Jesus is offering, and even who Jesus is, when instead, and depending on the intonation one brings to the question, "how can these things be?" might just as well indicate resistance. Nicodemus is unwilling to concede his religious authority, even though obedience to God was central to Judaism. In this regard, Jesus is requiring Nicodemus to shift his perspective of where power is located. Because of Jesus, the power of God is no longer found in the temple and its religious institutionalism but in the Word made flesh.

Another portion of the passage that lends itself to new perspectives from a postcolonial viewpoint is the phrase "kingdom of God." Compared to John's Synoptic counterparts, the phrase "kingdom of God" is a rare occurrence in the Gospel of John, appearing only here in chapter 3, "no one can see the kingdom of God without being born from above," and "no one can enter the kingdom of God without being born of water and Spirit" (vv. 3, 5), and then in John's passion narrative, "my kingdom is not from this world" (18:36).

Interpretive conclusions have most frequently connected "kingdom of God" in John 3 with salvation. One needs to be born again to receive salvation from God. A postcolonial lens recasts this overtheologizing and situates "kingdom of God" within a colonized state. At stake in the dialogue between Jesus and Nicodemus is indeed a question of allegiance—to what kingdom will one be loyal? In what light, in what fashion, do we imagine the kingdom of God, especially when displays of the might of that kingdom have already been decentered by a wedding in Cana and the temple of Jesus' body?

That the phrase "kingdom of God" is then next linked to Jesus' death in the passion narrative underscores what empire does when it is threatened in any way. It eliminates the threat. The use of "kingdom of God" in Jesus' trial before Pilate emphasizes the competing powers at work. In the end, the religious authorities are given the same choice as Nicodemus, and they choose Rome. It is a tragic moment theologically when the religious authorities are unable to recognize God's revelation in Jesus. But it is also a poignant moment for the occupied who sacrifice their obedience to God for their safety and security living as a colony of Rome. It is a choice of obedience to the colonizer, "We have no king but the emporer" (19:15), and perhaps the only choice they could make.

HOMILETICAL IMPLICATIONS

When considering the homiletical implications of a postcolonial interpretive perspective, we need first to consider how our preaching is "vulnerable to the insistent voice of colonialism/imperialism." Because empire is an inescapable context, a decolonizing homiletic begins with awareness, attention, and intention to the permeation of imperial tactics. We might ask, therefore, "What is the role of the pulpit in disrupting this discourse and participating in the decolonization of church and society?" At the same time, we must ask ourselves, "How am I held captive by empire? What power dynamics are present in the congregation by virtue of gender, race, economics, colonial/imperial experience? How is power used by others within the congregation? How do various listeners perceive my authority? How does my knowledge of my subject matter, my knowledge of listeners function as a weapon of power?" As the pulpit historically has been used to assert power, to control, and to oppress, embodying a postcolonial interpretive perspective is a first step toward the decolonization of preaching and worship. Preachers can make a commitment to decolonizing their preaching, which means "recognizing difference and diversity within the listening community and beyond, naming colonialism/imperialism as a past and present reality, speaking against the damaging and destructive patterns and discourses that have emerged within colonial/imperial projects, and coming to terms with the relationship between church and empire."[29]

Decolonizing our preaching can also happen in sermon preparation when we engage in decentering activities and seek out "decentering perspectives." Our work with the biblical texts, then, begins with acknowledging that the "Bible has been used as a weapon of colonial/imperial power."[30] It is a preacher's responsibility to articulate this truth, holding up examples of how the Bible is continually wielded to secure subjugation, uniformity, and control over and against minoritized persons, especially women, persons of color, and LGBTQIA+ persons. White Christian nationalism uses the Bible to justify superiority, privilege, Islamophobia, and anti-Semitism. Even when preachers speak out against this misuse, they are employing a postcolonial hermeneutic. We can also communicate in our preaching that the interpretation we are offering for this time and place is only one possibility, thereby speaking out against the hegemony of authoritative interpretation itself.

Postcolonial perspectives for biblical interpretation can be useful for preachers in navigating the tumultuous waters stirred up by the ebb and flow between politics and pulpit. The oft-used phrase "politics don't belong in the pulpit" renders too many preachers silent within the din of imperial atrocities. Preachers who risk challenging systems of empire such as racism, sexism, and heteronormativity are branded as too political. When politics is misconstrued as partisanship, the gospel itself becomes an apolitical movement. And yet, when politics is more broadly defined as "the total complex of relations between people living in society,"[31] the gospel is deeply political. Jesus challenged the organizational systems of his society, particularly those systems that exercised dominating and oppressive power. The first object of Jesus' critique was, of course, the Roman Empire. Neglecting the fact that Palestine in the first century was a Roman province skews Jesus' ministry and teachings toward only theological concerns, which are usually and conveniently our own theological issues, or representative of Christianity already years in the making.

Jesus spoke, Jesus preached, as a colonized person and as a citizen of a colonized community and state. To hear Jesus' words from this perspective gives preachers today a template for how to speak out against unchecked power or neo-colonizing efforts. Jesus himself becomes a model for political preaching that tells the truth of the gospel as a message seeking to undermine imperialism. Postcolonial criticism helps preachers articulate how the good news of Jesus Christ indeed has societal implications. Jesus' ministry and preaching did not bracket out critique of corrupt political systems, somehow bifurcating theology and justice. Rather, theology *is* justice.

Postcolonial interpretation exposes our homiletical inclinations to talk about God in the abstract and to equate theology with doctrines or dogmas decided long ago in denominational quarrels. For Jesus, theology was not systematic theology, but God actively moving the world toward righteousness. Postcolonial interpretation exposes our proclivities toward colonizing theology.

A preacher cannot preach about the "kingdom of God" without having some sense of how that phrase challenged the imperial realities of Jesus' day. Jesus' speech about the "kingdom of God," especially a kingdom that hungers and thirsts for righteousness, is resistance speech. Jesus sets forth a kingdom reality that is over and against the kingdom realities of Roman imperialism. To say "Christ reigns" is also to say that Caesar does not, which is dangerous speech indeed. Preaching about God's reign was a direct challenge to those in power in Jesus' day and called for action that would lead to punishment by said powers. "To preach the good news of God's kingdom is to speak a resounding 'no' to discourses that seek to dominate, separate, and homogenize others."[32]

Postcolonial criticism reminds preachers, and therefore faithful followers of Jesus, that the Jesus movement was a movement of the colonized, not of those having any kind of power. One of the reasons that Jesus' authority is consistently questioned in the four Gospels is not just to secure a connection between Jesus and God but also to set Jesus' power over and against the power of the Roman Empire. It is an important reminder that Christianity did not begin as a belief system of the powerful but as a fringe movement of the powerless. Even after Christianity's origins in Palestine as an intra-Jewish movement, it took hold in Gentile communities, and thus became a construct for outsiders. We were once the Gentiles—postcolonialism demands a long, hard look in the mirror.

Jesus' critique of political, social, religious, institutional, and cultural systems is done for the sake of exposing their dominance. Preachers have a mandate, therefore, to do the same in their preaching. Silence in these matters risks complacency and complicity with regard to unjust practices that seek only to domesticate and control.

As Christianity has been presented and upheld in our society, linked to the so-called blessed and the prosperous, and as a religion of the successful and the resourceful, postcolonialism gives the preacher the theoretical base to call out such falsehoods. Postcolonial interpretation puts a mirror before the church and "the manner in which empires, small and large, have sought to manage relationship and maintain power and control."[33] The "hallmarks of colonizing discourse" as "domination, separation, homogeneity, fixedness"[34] are widely found in ecclesial discourse. Furthermore, postcolonial interpretation exposes how we have conveniently forgotten the hegemony of the Christian church, first as the religion of the empire, and then as an arm of empire into missionary outposts for the sake of the spread of the gospel. Christianity and "civilizing mission" actively engaged in colonization.[35] The church cannot exist in the world today without realizing the effects of empire on its past, present, and future. "Worship spaces are inhabited by both (formerly) colonizing and (formerly) colonized peoples as well as observers, all of whom live in a nation that continues to be affected by imperial forces and participates in colonial discourses."[36] In a world still gripped by the lures of empire, the church is an essential model of and voice for liberating proclamation.

FURTHER RESOURCES FOR PREACHING

Kim-Cragg, Hyeran. *Postcolonial Preaching: Creating a Ripple Effect.* Lanham, MD: Lexington Books, 2021.

Travis, Sarah. *Decolonizing Preaching: The Pulpit as Postcolonial Space.* Eugene, OR: Cascade Books, 2014.

3

Feminist Interpretation

INTRODUCTION

Feminist interpretation of the Bible has been a critical component of biblical scholarship for the last forty years.[1] Of course, women have been reading the Bible for centuries, but attention to how women read Scripture as women is what demarcates feminist scholarship on the Bible. Like other approaches and methodologies in biblical interpretation, feminist interpretation cannot be succinctly defined, because feminist interpreters, like any interpreters of Scripture, are as varied as the interpretations themselves. Consciousness of how women read the Bible, and how interpretations of the Bible led to the harm of women, date to the late nineteenth and early twentieth centuries' first-wave feminism and such pioneers as Elizabeth Cady Stanton and Sojourner Truth. The advent of second-wave feminism, the women's liberation movement in the 1960s to 1980s, would bring these feminist concerns into the scholarly academy.

Third-wave feminism (1990s) lodged the important critique that not all self-identified feminists are on equal footing. While early feminist criticism in biblical scholarship provided much-needed perspective on and correction of biblical scholarship that had been dominated by white, European male figures, the first waves of feminist interpretation in biblical studies lacked the kind of diversity that we see in scholarship today. Early stages of feminism,[2] and thus feminist biblical criticism, represented mostly highly educated, white, cisgender, middle-class North American women who normalized their perspectives.

Current trends in feminist biblical interpretation recognize the importance that intersectionality, or intersectional feminism, brings to any feminist scholarship. Womanist (African American), *mujerista* (Latinx), lesbian, and trans interpreters have critiqued feminist interpretation of the Bible for inadequately tending to the many levels and layers that comprise identity: "race, ethnicity, language, culture, and sexuality."[3] For example, womanism as "black women's feminism . . . distinguishes itself from the dominant-culture feminism, which is all too often distorted by racism and classism and marginalizes womanism, womanists, and women of color."[4] As an example of intersectional critique of the feminist movement, womanist interpretation thus names its own complexities.

> Womanism is often simply defined as black feminism. It is that, and it is much more. It is a richer, deeper, liberative paradigm; a social, cultural, and political space and theological matrix with the experiences and multiple identities of black women at the center. Womanism shares the radical egalitarianism that characterizes feminism at its basic level, but without its default referent, white women functioning as the exemplar for all women.[5]

In this regard, "African American women have challenged or resisted feminism. The challenges include: (1) feminism lacked a 'class' agenda; (2) feminism lacked a message for men and women in community; (3) feminism ignored racism; (4) feminist theology did not value religious experience; and (5) feminism ignored issues of gender identity."[6] Intersectional feminism realizes that many factors contribute to the oppression of and discrimination against women, including, but not exhausted by, gender identity, race, class, sexual orientation, ethnicity, ability, age, religion, and socioeconomic status. As a result, within these subsets of feminism, there is not a uniform definition or approach.[7] How these factors also intersect in a biblical text becomes an important interpretive commitment. Intersectionality is our reality. No human being exists in a one-dimensional bubble. In the case of womanism, for example, Stephanie Buckhanon Crowder summarizes,

> Womanist thinking is an interpretive approach that takes into account the role of race, gender, and class, among other ontological factors, in the lives of African American women. Womanist

hermeneutics interrogates and analyzes the roles assigned to African American or African Diasporan women by their families and the dominant culture, the persistent stereotypes about African American women, the impact of race with gender and class (my addition), and the diversity among women.[8]

How the preacher acknowledges the truth of intersectionality, both in the writings of the Bible and in our lives, is critical for faithful interpretation of Scripture and faithful exegesis of the human condition. Any feminist perspective must also include an awareness of the "default referent" in feminism that privileges the experiences of white women.

SUMMARY OF THE APPROACH

In general, feminist interpretation of the Bible raises essential questions about the power, authority, and use of Scripture. "It seeks to enable women to locate their own places in Christian history, to argue for changes in ecclesial practice and doctrine, and to find personal inspiration."[9] Essential to feminist approaches is calling out the patriarchy and androcentrism that continue to dominate biblical scholarship. Patriarchy is any system in which men have the primary power and domination. Androcentrism assumes a male worldview as normative for society. When women read the Bible, they bring to these writings different perspectives that had been overlooked or ignored for centuries. When women read the Bible, they hear themselves somewhere in the margins, they speak up for those silenced, and they tell the truth when patriarchal approaches to the Bible continue to harm the faithful and lead astray the searching.

Biblical scholars who have delineated their approaches as feminist represent a wide spectrum of methods brought to interpreting the Bible.[10] As noted above, womanist biblical interpretation, for example, "holds gender dynamics, race matters, and class systems to the light,"[11] as well as how patriarchal ecclesial institutions continue to oppress women. While feminism in biblical scholarship, therefore, engages in many facets of biblical interpretation, it also testifies to the ways in which different forms and degrees of oppression are brought to and result from the interpretation of biblical texts. It makes sense, then, that feminist criticism of the Bible presents a variety of methodological concerns and approaches.

Some feminists will find the means to salvage a biblical text as Scripture. In other words, these scholars take canonicity seriously, agreeing that the books in the library we call the Bible were deemed Scripture by the church and therefore are a primary source for theological reflection and, we might add, the basis for sermons. On the other end of the spectrum are feminist scholars who outright reject a biblical passage or book, deemed not worthy of study because of the damage it has done historically. "No text that is destructive of the human and personal worth of women (or anyone else) can be the revealed word of God."[12] Being aware of this range of approaches in feminist criticism and interpretation of the Bible is essential for the preacher. Recognizing the particular critique at work in feminist interpretation will help the preacher discern and determine the appropriate homiletical direction to take for a specific sermon.

Amy-Jill Levine provides a helpful summary of the various questions asked by feminist interpreters:[13]

1. "Can women's voices or lives be recovered from this text? Can the text's impact on women be determined? To what extent is the text prescriptive rather than descriptive, and to what extent does it suppress or reveal?"

2. How "do women characters achieve their goals? Are they coded as deceitful or forthright, meek or strident, in positions of authority or subservience?"

3. "How are metaphors of female experiences . . . depicted, and to what ends?"

4. "Can the text be read 'against the grain' in order to find 'good news'?"

5. "How are pericopes titled and people labeled?" How are labels "determined by gender-based considerations"?

6. "What are the implications of named vs. anonymous characters, and how can unidentified figures be recovered?"

7. What political or ideological interests (such as the inherent patriarchy and androcentrism of Scripture) are encoded in the text? "How might the application of the 'hermeneutics of suspicion' . . . reveal such interests?"

8. "How does the social location of the reader impact interpretation?"

Feminist interpreters who focus on construction when it comes to the interpretation of the Bible tend to focus their studies on four areas of approach. Exploring female images for God and bringing out stories of women in Scripture is the first strategy used by feminist interpreters to construct different views of, and yet valid perspectives from, the Bible's intrinsic androcentrism and patriarchy. Tending female images for God is particularly important for preaching in that a faithful homiletic is one that regularly seeks to expand theological imagination. Second, feminist interpreters highlight the historical and social roles of women in biblical times so that experiences and perspectives of women might be "reconstructed." Locating the biblical texts in their historical, societal, political, and religious contexts thus denormalizes biblical womanhood. Third, while men have indeed dominated the history of interpretation of the Bible, they have not been the only interpreters of Scripture. Highlighting women interpreters of Scripture throughout the two thousand years of scholarship on the Bible is a third approach by which to recover women's voices in biblical scholarship.[14] Finally, a feminist interpreter will ask the direct question, How does the meaning of a text change when women read?

Certainly not all approaches can be used at the same time to engage a biblical text, especially when the intended result is a sermon. At the same time, awareness of these different trajectories in feminist interpretation will lead to desperately needed alternative viewpoints on passages too long held captive by male-dominated concerns and objectives.

SAMPLE TEXT: JOHN 4:1–42

A feminist critique of the story of the woman at the well[15] first locates this passage within the larger context of John's narrative, specifically as the next encounter between Jesus and a character following the conversation between Nicodemus and Jesus. Side by side, the contrast between Nicodemus and the Samaritan woman is striking: Nicodemus is a Pharisee, a leader of the Jews, a man with religious, political, and social power. She is a woman with no name, a Samaritan, a religious and political outsider. The conversation with Nicodemus takes place in Jerusalem, the religious center of Judaism in the first century. The dialogue between the Samaritan woman and Jesus happens in Sychar, in the middle of Samaria, a region that Jews would avoid for fear of contact with Samaritans, thereby becoming ritually unclean. Nicodemus comes to Jesus by night, and night or darkness in the Gospel of John symbolizes unbelief and not being in a relationship with Jesus.

The woman at the well, however, meets Jesus at noon, the lightest, brightest time of day, when the sun is the highest in the sky, intimating that she has the potential to be in the kind of relationship with Jesus to which every character in the narrative is invited. Commentators still insist that she, as a recognized sinner among her townspeople, comes to the well at noon to avoid meeting up with other women in the village and the shame and blame associated with such an encounter. It could have been, however, that she simply needed more water to complete her domestic responsibilities. Sexism and misogyny blur the capacity to recognize the purpose and meaning of the imagery of light and darkness in the Fourth Gospel.

Established expectations would suggest Nicodemus is the superior conversation partner for Jesus, and yet a comparison of the length of each conversation alludes otherwise. In fact, the conversation between Jesus and the Samaritan woman at the well is the longest conversation Jesus has with someone in all four Gospels. Mapping the dialogue between Jesus and Nicodemus and then between Jesus with the woman at the well, there is a similar pattern: an initial exchange, followed by misunderstanding of Jesus' words and identity, and then conversation. Nicodemus's part of the conversation is one brief response, "How can these things be?" (3:9), with the rest of the encounter being a monologue from Jesus. For Jesus and the woman at the well, their conversation continues, and she ends up testifying to her fellow villagers about her encounter with Jesus, modeling what witness looks like.

In this juxtaposition of Nicodemus and the woman at the well, the Fourth Evangelist suggests an unconventional reading of this unnamed Samaritan woman. Not only is the woman at the well on equal footing with Nicodemus—she surpasses him. The Samaritan woman at the well experiences equality and liberation, thereby denormalizing texts that have been used to justify oppression or subjugation of and domination over women. A sermon on this passage from a feminist interpretive perspective could first make mention of this unexpected characterization.

Tracking the conversation further, the woman at the well and Jesus model open and truthful dialogue. "They are not talking past one another but to one another."[16] When the woman recognizes that Jesus is the source of what she came to the well for in the first place, water (John 4:15), Jesus acknowledges her insight by moving the conversation forward. In her honest response about her marital status and with the exchange that follows, the woman then understands Jesus to be a prophet. He is a prophet not because he can predict the future, but a prophet in the true sense of the Old Testament prophets. God's prophets were truth tellers, naming the realities of the behavior and circumstances of God's people to bring the Israelites back into righteous relationship with God. Jesus knows her truth and tells her, just like the prophets of old.

In the wider context of the Fourth Gospel, a similar pattern occurs in the healing of the man born blind, in chapter 9. The man born blind, in the conversation and interrogations with the Pharisees that follow his healing, also realizes that Jesus is a prophet (v. 17; see also 6:14). Eventually, the man born blind states that Jesus must be from God (9:33) and identifies Jesus *as* God when he worships Jesus (v. 38). This gradual recognition of Jesus' identity is the same for the woman at the well. After realizing that Jesus is a prophet, she then wonders if he is the Messiah (4:29).

Rather than hold up this narrative pattern in John, some commentators on this passage still insist that Jesus' request of the woman at the well, "Go, call your husband," is to expose her sin of immoral behavior instead of getting her to the next step of acknowledging Jesus' identity. Thus, feminist interpretation of the story would acknowledge and name how, in both sermons and commentaries, this woman remains a victim of misogyny and contemporary sexism. Many preachers (and listeners, for that matter) can recall having heard a sermon on, or even still assume themselves, the supposed sinfulness of the woman at the well and her debauched behavior. That she has had five husbands is presumed to be her fault, that she has gone from man to man, cannot keep a man, is promiscuous, or has a rather loose view of marriage. This is only confirmed by the fact that she is now living with a man who is not her husband, therefore clearly living in sin outside marriage.

Commentators suggest that because she admits the truth about her marital situation—she does not have a husband—Jesus then forgives her of her sin, which is, of course, nowhere to be found in the text. In this patriarchal mind-set, the women's question to Jesus about where to worship (John 4:20) is her way of deflecting the conversation or shifting the focus away from her sin. In changing the subject, she admits her guilt. A feminist critique names this misinterpretation as biased reading based on our modern patriarchal and sexist societal constructions of women. Underneath this interpretation lie the assumptions that women are overtly sexual; that women are at fault for failed relationships; that women are "loose" if they marry more than once; that this woman "can't keep her man"; and that women are not capable of intelligent conversation, especially with a man. It is because of her truth telling, however, "I have no husband" (v. 17), that Jesus speaks his truth, "I am he, the one who is speaking to you" (v. 26). This is the first absolute "I am" statement in the Gospel of John—and it is for her.[17] Furthermore, in saying, "I have no husband," the woman "steps free from her situation. . . . In this moment she makes the decision to become independent of this man." In this exchange with Jesus, she realizes what is possible. "She cannot become a spring of living water if she continues to live in her dependence on a man who exploits her."[18]

A feminist approach to biblical interpretation can provide a critique of past interpretations that have perpetuated the patriarchy already inherent in biblical texts. Offering a corrective is often a necessary homiletical goal, especially for passages that have had a history of misuse and abuse, even a legacy of incorrect readings. As noted above, feminism highlights the historical and social roles of women in biblical times as one strategy for interpretation. Feminism, like any of the approaches presented in this book, does not eschew the historical-critical method. To be sure, one of the tasks of the preacher is to locate these stories within their original contexts of meaning. We are responsible for historical-critical study of the biblical writings that is then faithful to the times and issues from which these writings originated. To ignore this responsibility leads to erroneous readings and unfaithful preaching.

Careful historical-critical study of this passage yields the truth about this woman's situation. First-century women had few rights, especially when it came to relationships, marriage, and divorce. Why would this woman have had five husbands? They either died or divorced her. The number of husbands also indicates her need to remarry, because the woman at the well did not have a son. Without her husband's heir, without someone to take care of her, she is dependent on remarrying for her livelihood and survival. Women could not initiate a divorce, but a husband was permitted to divorce his wife for the most benign of reasons. The primary reason for a man to divorce his wife in first-century Palestine was because she had not produced an heir and therefore was assumed to be barren. The inability to have children was never, of course, a man's fault.

The Samaritan woman living with a man to whom she is not married is not equivalent to a contemporary couple living together prior to marriage. "Shacking up" was not a first-century option. Rather, historical-critical research reveals that her situation is most likely a levirate marriage. According to God's law, in Deuteronomy 25:5–10, if a man's brother died and there was no heir, the man was obligated to bring in the wife of his dead brother and marry her, either formally or in an informal agreement. Often, the first child between them would be accounted to the deceased brother/husband to carry on his name.

Women were consistently at risk for survival, particularly if they were not married. To some extent, therefore, the woman at the well was "obliged to marry repeatedly for economic and social reasons. Her situation was so grave that she was forced to enter a nonmarital working and sexual relationship with a man who did not even bother to give her the relative security of a marriage contract."[19] Resituating the story of the woman at the well into its historical context liberates her from a sentence of supposed sinfulness, shame, and blame.

Feminist interpretation lifts up passages in Scripture where women seem to experience equality and liberation. In the contrast between Nicodemus and the Samaritan woman at the well, she, and not Nicodemus, is the first exemplar in the Fourth Gospel of a key characteristic of discipleship—witness. In fact, this is her call story. "In the history of exegesis, the tendency at all costs to overlook this call narrative has been powerful and conspicuous."[20] Following her encounter with Jesus, she does not stay silent but returns to her townspeople, risking rejection for sure—we can't forget that she was talking with a Jew—and perhaps even Roman punishment for aligning herself with Jewish messianism. The woman invites the villagers to "come and see" this Jesus who told her everything she had ever done (John 4:28–30). "Come and see" are the very same words that Jesus uses to invite his first disciples to follow him (1:39). The Samaritan woman, therefore, is calling new disciples to follow Jesus, and we are told that some of her fellow townspeople answer her invitation and go to Jesus. "They left the city and were on their way to him" (4:30). In their own personal encounter with Jesus, these Samaritans then end up confessing the truth of Jesus' identity, "This is truly the Savior of the world" (v. 42), a confession that is found nowhere else in the entire Gospel of John. This is the first and only time the word "savior" is used in the Fourth Gospel. Were it not for the invitation of the woman at the well, "come and see," these Samaritans would still be in darkness and still be thirsty. The Samaritan woman at the well becomes one "who passes on living water to others."[21]

Feminist interpretation of the Bible is also intentional about reading the text from the perspective of female characters or persons who are oppressed and marginalized. When we imagine the viewpoint of the woman at the well, what she has experienced in her life would mean overwhelming shame and blame. Her plight, her marital situation, and her inability to give her husbands an heir would be considered a triple curse caused by either her sin or the sins of her ancestors (no wonder she was forced to go to the well alone—who wants to be around her, having her sin rub off on them?).[22] Having had five husbands would be both disgraceful and dishonoring, an indignity exacerbated by the fact that she could not fulfill the one role that was her purpose in life—to bear children.

From the perspective of intersectionality, her levels of discrimination and oppression are multiple—she is a woman, a religious minority, unmarried, and without children. And yet, Jesus goes to Sychar to find her. "He had to go through Samaria" (4:4), a verse omitted from the Revised Common Lectionary. A more accurate translation of the Greek, dei, would be, "It was necessary for him to go through Samaria." There is no geographical reason to pass through Samaria when traveling from Jerusalem to Galilee. In fact, no Jew would go through Samaria because that would mean coming in contact with a Samaritan. Jesus' decision to take a route that leads him and his disciples to Samaria is a theological necessity based on John 3:16, "For God so loved the world that he gave his only Son, so that everyone who believes in him may not perish but may have eternal life." Jesus is fulfilling his mission, God's mission, to love the entire world. The disciples need to know, we need to know, what this world looks like, and the world God loves is indeed a woman whom the world has dismissed.

HOMILETICAL IMPLICATIONS

The homiletical payoffs of feminist biblical interpretation of passages for preaching are far-reaching. For women who have had the Bible used against them to justify abuse, to tell them to remain in an abusive relationship, to validate patriarchal structures, or to authorize objectification of women, this approach might very well redeem the Bible as Scripture for them once again. Hearing from the pulpit the importance of women's roles in witnessing to Jesus as Messiah and Savior will be both life-giving and liberating. Women might believe that their place in the history of God's people has always been on equal footing with men, regardless of how our culture and the church have told them otherwise. Women might actually hear themselves in the pages of Scripture, voices too long silenced.[23] Women might actually believe that God, that the church, is for them and not against them.

Half of our congregations are made up of women, and yet, how often do preachers intentionally raise up women's voices from Scripture or focus sermons on the particular perspectives of what women hear and read in the Bible? A feminist perspective might also investigate lectionary passages and omissions. Who is left out? A preacher might consider a sermon series on the lost women of the Bible. Or, a preacher might bring a critique to those passages that are used to uphold and justify affliction as a theological demand. "Feminist readers mark texts not specifically addressed to women, but which have been read as oppressive to women (and others) by glorifying suffering and encouraging victimization instead of resistance."[24] When we do not pay attention to the ways in which women interpret the Bible, we are leaving out a significant number of our believers and their unique voices in envisioning the kingdom of God.

Feminist interpretation is committed to a profound understanding and regard of the other. When we preach in a way that models how to embody acts of liberation, we invite our listeners to imagine that possibility in their own lives. When we free the characters in Scripture from the bondage of misogynist, sexist, and patriarchal interpretation, we are also freeing persons in our pews from the same and freeing them for more open, generous, and life-giving views of Scripture, of God, of one another, and of themselves.

Feminist interpretation challenges the assumptions behind hermeneutics, in particular a white, male, cis, Anglo-Saxon hermeneutic that has dominated modern biblical scholarship. It is critical for the preacher to demonstrate on a regular basis how quickly any hermeneutic can be viewed as divine or divinely sanctioned if it is never brought under any kind of critical scrutiny. Without such scrutiny, too often God's intention and God's voice are placed behind words never said by God. Our own interpretive enterprises demand regular self-examination so that we do not equate the voices of the biblical authors with the voice of God.

Feminist interpretation points out the embedded theological commitments we bring to the interpretation of biblical texts, even though we rarely name or admit those commitments. We do not just read the Bible as descriptive of God and of how to live life as a believer. We engage in constant interplay between what the Bible says, what we think it says, what we want it to say, and how all of that lines up, or does not, with our experiences of God. Feminist interpretation of the Bible names the truth of our dominant images for God and from where these images originate. It names the truth that all too often our images of God trump the witness of biblical texts.

When preachers call attention to passages that can directly refute texts used to silence and oppress women, we raise the important issue of how biblical theology, denominations, and professions of faith all operate with a canon within a canon, allowing some passages to have more authority than others. Why and how is it that the story of the Samaritan woman at the well is bypassed in favor of upholding 1 Timothy 2:12, "I permit no woman to teach or to have authority over a man; she is to keep silent," as normative? How will preachers use biblical stories that liberate women to speak up against the texts used to oppress them? It is a troubling phenomenon that the biblical passages cited to justify suppression and submission of women[25] eclipse those stories where Jesus' ministry is dependent on them. Feminist interpretation investigates the nature of the authority given to passages (and their skewed interpretations). How preachers address the question and concept of biblical authority from the pulpit is a critical issue when the nature of the Bible's authority is not uniformly understood or even accepted.

Feminist interpretation gives preachers the skills to develop and nurture theological imagination when engaging the Bible and when making sense of the world through the lens of God's assumed activity in it. Much preaching suffers from reductionist theology or theology too readily prescribed by denominational and confessional commitments. We forget that claims, creeds, and confessions for which we argue based on the Bible, "the Bible says," reveal our presuppositions of God. We cannot separate our embedded theology from how and why we use Scripture the way we do. Feminist interpretation of the Bible succeeds in challenging our constructions of God, particularly our gendered readings of God. Recapturing female imagery of God expands our capacities to imagine God's identity and God's activity beyond androcentric portrayals of God. Preaching on women characters in Scripture communicates the diversity of God's reign and the need of God for all persons in bringing about the promises of the kingdom of God. When the voices of women are heard from the pages of Scripture, the witnesses to God's love, grace, mercy, and salvation double. If we pay attention to only half of the population in the Bible, we have consequentially abridged God's revelation.

Finally, when the preacher uses feminist interpretation to read the Bible for preaching, the preacher is exercising the prophetic voice. Prophetic preaching is preaching that is willing to tell the truth, the truth about God, but also the truth about the human condition, and, especially, the truth about how the church regularly uses God and our religious institutions to justify or hide systemic sexism and misogyny. The underrepresentation of women in higher leadership roles in the church persists. Systemic abuse of women by men in leadership roles in the church continues to be brought to light. Women in ministry are daily met with both overt and covert questioning of their fitness for ministry.[26] Preachers are called to exercise their authority to speak out against the oppression of women and to speak up and be allies, especially for women in light of the #MeToo and #ChurchToo movements. To read and preach the Bible as a feminist results in nothing short of redemption for all.

FURTHER RESOURCES FOR PREACHING

Gross, Nancy Lammers. *Women's Voices and the Practice of Preaching.* Grand Rapids: Eerdmans, 2017.

Kim, Eunjoo Mary. *Women Preaching: Theology and Practice through the Ages.* Eugene, OR: Wipf & Stock, 2009.

Lauve-Moon, Katie. *Preacher Woman: A Critical Look at Sexism without Sexists.* Oxford: Oxford University Press, 2021.

Thompson, Lisa. *Ingenuity: Preaching as an Outsider.* Nashville: Abingdon Press, 2018.

Tisdale, Leonora Tubbs. *How Women Transform Preaching.* Nashville: Abingdon Press, 2021.

4

African American Interpretation

INTRODUCTION

The essential feature of African American biblical interpretation is the distinctiveness of the African American experience, and yet, "any attempt to outline the broad parameters of an African American use of the Bible must be qualified with words on the order of non-monolithic, multifaceted, and diverse."[1] The entirety of the history of Black persons in America is then brought to bear in making sense of how the Bible speaks here and now.[2] Histories narrate past time but have a marked influence on our present lives. In the case of the Black experience in America, it is history itself that is forgotten in the contest for power evident in white supremacy and white privilege. Yet, it is the very history of African Americans that overlaps and mirrors biblical history.

The Bible, and especially the books of the Old Testament or Hebrew Bible, tells a story of oppression. It tells a story of a people, God's people, enslaved by foreign powers and then freed by the hand of God. "It is the story of the exodus of Israel from Egyptian bondage (Exod 14) that continues to serve as the primary liberation motif for black Christians."[3] As such, the Bible itself is a liberating text—it is not just about liberation but has the power to liberate when read and preached through the lens of emancipation. "The macrostory of the exodus is the story of the journey from *bondage* to *freedom*" where "humanity's great need here is not for forgiveness or reconciliation, but for freedom. With this in mind, "the problem facing the children of Israel in Egypt was not that they were *sinful*; it was that they were *slaves*."[4]

African American biblical interpretation has been an especially important critic of biblical scholarship historically dominated by white, European, male interpretation. While all interpretation is subjective, subjectivity does not always result in the reflective capacity to critique subjectivity. In the case of biblical interpretation, the readings held as accurate, critical, even objective, were and still are those determined by white male privilege. As whiteness itself has occupied authority in biblical scholarship, Black experience becomes even more essential, both for unmasking white supremacy and for naming underrepresented, even unnoticed, scriptural themes. In the favoring of whiteness, "they would have us believe it is a mere and fortuitous coincidence that the meaning they would unearth is a meaning that applies to the needs and concerns of the space they happen to occupy."[5] African American biblical interpretation challenges the universalization of white, male methodology, then giving hermeneutical voice to the poor and the oppressed. In the same Bible that is used to justify "untold harm on Black people," Black Christians have seen "the basis for their dignity and hope in a culture that often denied them both."[6]

Furthermore, African American biblical interpretation provides an important corrective to the triumphalism of mainstream Christianity bent on protecting the status quo.[7] A focus on the resurrection leads to a different assessment of Jesus' ministry and death than attention to the crucifixion. When the crucifixion is fixed in view, we can no longer ignore the injustice of Jesus' torture and death. We can no longer overlook the fact that before the cross was a symbol of salvation and a promise of the forgiveness of sins, it was an indictment of empire—those systems and institutions that will keep their power at any cost. The cross exposed what imperialism does when it perceives a threat—it eliminates the source that would speak out against it.

SUMMARY OF THE APPROACH

"To be black in America is not a singular thing; accordingly there is no singular black biblical interpretation."[8] One African American approach to biblical interpretation begins with the incarnation, reflecting the historical offensive on the African American body. "In a negrophobic society, black ontological integrity suffers compromise. On the one hand, massive, negative, transgenerational assault on black bodies has ontological implications. In such a society, blackness mutates as negation, nonbeing, nothingness; blackness insinuates an 'other' so radically different that her and his very humanity is discredited."[9] It is the humanity of Jesus that promises and points to God's solidarity with Black suffering. Jesus is seen, then, "as a man in history, marked by his particularity as a son of Israel and by his marginality as a subject under the domination of Greek culture and Roman imperialism in first-century Palestine."[10] While no human can be free of suffering, the suffering of Black persons is exacerbated by slavery, discrimination, and racism. In Jesus is God's continuing commitment to the liberation of the oppressed so that the Bible's liberating story stands in direct contrast to the enchainment of slavery.

African American interpretation reads "the Bible for freedom— freedom from racist ideologies supporting their enslavement, from oppressive interpretations of the biblical text, and from hermeneutical constructions of a God and Jesus who despise black people. They read for freedom from spiritual, emotional/psychological, social and physical bondage."[11] The heart of God beats of freedom toward emancipation, not only of literal persons and communities but also from sin and evil, especially evil, "concretized in racial exclusivity and the dehumanization of the poor."[12] It is this unfettering lens that identifies African American biblical interpretation. As a result, central to African American engagement with Scripture is an actual encounter with Scripture that is then "wed . . . to the lived experience of the black congregation."[13]

Furthermore, the Bible is a compendium of stories of the oppressed. "The Bible, through the words and actions of Jesus Christ, glorifies people groups of similar circumstances, such as the poor, widow, prostitutes, tax collectors, lepers, Samaritans, and others ostracized from the general community. Essentially, African Americans find it very easy to identify with those people who, like themselves, have had to fight for recognition from their oppressors."[14]

An African American approach to the interpretation of Scripture for preaching pays attention to themes that "speak to African-American space."[15] Emerson Powery asserts that "fundamental to any 'black' approach to any biblical text are the notions of liberation, resistance, *and* survival."[16] The most prominent themes include, but are not limited to, slavery and liberation, social justice, care for the whole community (not simply a single soul's salvation), freedom from oppression, and God's solidarity with the oppressed, especially Jesus' solidarity with the poor by suffering on their behalf.

African American interpretation of Scripture lends a larger scope to the meaning of salvation. "Salvation is broken spirits being healed, voiceless people speaking out, and black people empowered to love their own blackness."[17] As Cone notes, Black slaves "ignored white theology, which did not affirm their humanity, and went straight to stories in the Bible, interpreting them as stories of God siding with the little people just like them. They identified God's liberation of the poor as the central message of the Bible."[18] African American preaching thus also pays attention to Black characters in the Bible. "Who were the Cushites, the Nabateans, the Egyptians, and other African peoples in the Bible? Where were Cyrene, Niger, Sheba, and other locations that are mentioned? Who were the Queen of Sheba (1 Kings 10:1–3), Zipporah (Exod. 2:21; Num. 12:1), Ebed-melech (Jer. 38:7–13), Hagar (Gen. 16:1–3), Simon of Cyrene (Mark 15:21), and the Ethiopian eunuch (Acts 8:27–39)?"[19]

A number of Black scholars reject the interpretation of the cross of Jesus as that which saved us from sin, with the correlate that we must suffer as Jesus did.[20] As central as the cross can be with regard to Jesus' solidarity, African American interpretation takes the spotlight away from the cross as the locus of salvation and refocuses salvation as Jesus' solidarity with suffering that led to the cross,[21] standing existentially at the foot of the cross. The good news that is the gospel has to be "more than a transcendent reality, more than 'going to heaven when I die, to shout salvation as I fly.' It is also an immanent reality—a powerful liberating presence among the poor right *now* in their midst." Without a concretization of God's presence in humiliation, in suffering, in the lives of the poor, "the gospel becomes simply an opiate."[22]

African American biblical interpretation, with the Black experience as the starting point, forces the interpretive enterprise to make the connection between the cross and the lynching tree. We look away from this juxtaposition at our own peril, for in doing so we are complicit in white supremacy. "Until we can see the cross and the lynching tree together, until we can identify Christ with a 'recrucified' black body hanging from a lynching tree, there can be no genuine understanding of Christian identity in America, and no deliverance from the brutal legacy of slavery and white supremacy."[23]

SAMPLE TEXT: JOHN 18:1–19:42

The passion narrative as told by the Gospel of John is the designated Gospel text for Good Friday.[24] Yet preaching on John's passion narrative is frequently not a priority, as other liturgical choices and rituals for Good Friday worship services often stand in competition with a sermon on the Gospel. Furthermore, the move of the church from a focus on Palm Sunday to an emphasis on Passion Sunday favors preaching on Jesus' crucifixion according to the Synoptic Gospels. The choice to dedicate a sermon to John's version of the events of Jesus' arrest, trial, and crucifixion needs to be intentional, or the preacher finds other homiletical opportunities to preach through John's passion narrative.[25]

At first glance, John's account of Jesus' unjust arrest, trial, death sentence, and execution may appear to have little resonance with the theological themes central to African American biblical interpretation. John's Jesus does not seem to suffer much, especially when compared to the crucifixion accounts in Matthew and Mark. It is in Matthew and Mark that Jesus utters the ultimate cry of suffering, giving voice to his abandonment and absolute anguish, "My God, my God, why have you forsaken me?" (Matt. 27:46; Mark 15:34). In contrast, the Jesus of John is in control, virtually unfazed by the events of his last hours of life: he willingly hands himself over to the authorities at his arrest (18:1–11), carries his own cross (19:17), takes care of his mother and the Beloved Disciple as he is hanging on the cross (vv. 26–27), asks for a drink before being offered one (v. 28), and announces a victorious ending (v. 30).

However, with an African American hermeneutic, the humanity of Jesus, especially the very human side of Jesus' death so often overlooked in the Fourth Gospel, comes to light. The triumphalism that frequently dominates readings of John's passion narrative is, in the end, not a truthful reading of a Gospel that places its primary christological focus on the incarnation, the Word become flesh (1:14). For Martin Luther King Jr., "the cross represented the depth of God's love for suffering humanity, and an answer to the deadly cycle of violence and hatred."[26] Considering this is the Gospel of John, "For God so loved the world that he gave his only Son, so that everyone who believes in him may not perish but may have eternal life" (3:16), the cross embodies this suffering love for the whole world.

With an African American perspective, it is Jesus' solidarity with humanity that comes into focus. Less attention on Jesus' suffering does not mean an absence of suffering, but that the meaning of the cross is aimed in an alternative direction. Much of Christian interpretation of Jesus' crucifixion has indeed fixated on the suffering of Jesus, suffering for the sake of forgiveness of sin or sins. And yet, this claim about the cross of Christ is not necessarily good news for the African American struggle. Jesus' suffering can have implications other than the personal release of guilt. With an African American lens, Jesus' suffering is indicative of what unchecked power does to voices that dare to speak out against it. "The cross was God's critique of power—white power—with powerless love, snatching victory out of defeat."[27] The cross in the Gospel of John, therefore, becomes a symbol of the hegemony of empire. In this regard, the crucifixion is not a salvific act in a narrowly construed theological sense. The cross exposes the ruthlessness of authorities that crush anything and anyone that might stand in the way of certain dominion and absolute rule. All too often, our preaching on the passion of Jesus devolves into theological generalisms or becomes "a magical talisman for salvation."[28] "We cannot find liberating joy in the cross by spiritualizing it, by taking away its message of justice in the midst of powerlessness, suffering, and death."[29]

With this view of the cross held up, the triumphalism of the crucifixion in John is reevaluated. A triumphalist interpretation of the cross of Jesus as it seems to appear in the Fourth Gospel has the propensity to set aside the very real affliction of Jesus, even downplaying Jesus' agony. In doing so, the humanity of Jesus is moderated at the very moment the humanity of Jesus should take center stage. A negation of the real suffering of Jesus furthermore undercuts the theological impulse of John, a Gospel that insists on holding Jesus as human and Jesus as divine in constant tension. For example, while one of Jesus' last words from the cross, "I thirst," can be an act of control, as mentioned in the above discussion, the very words indicate his humanity, suffering, and abandonment. He hangs on the cross desiccated, with no one offering him something to drink. Jesus has to beg for a sip to soothe his parched lips. The source of living water (4:14) is waterless.

An African American approach to the interpretation of John's passion narrative also avoids a sentimentalism of the cross that reduces Jesus' motions to mere scripted actions in a well-plotted divine play. An overemphasizing of Jesus' agency has the potential to conclude that Jesus' agony was not real and that his victimization was simply penned by the Fourth Evangelist. Jesus, who was from the beginning, from God, and with God (1:1), the Word made flesh, the I AM in the world, was indeed a victim of violence. That Jesus was a victim of violence is, then, the certainty of Jesus' solidarity with the Black plight. And this solidarity is all the more assured when preachers see the cross and the lynching tree together.

Cast in this light, a walk through the passion narrative in John surfaces alternative meanings for details typically construed as presenting a Jesus who barely seems human. Jesus' giving of himself over to the authorities at his arrest, and not being handed over by Judas with a kiss, is thus not triumphalism but rather an act of protest that exposes the absurdity of the moment. Standing outside the garden are hundreds of Roman soldiers[30] along with police from the chief priests and the Pharisees. Jesus has no chance against an entourage of power of these proportions. Jesus hands himself over to call out the excessiveness of empire that has to display its power as an impulse to assuage its own fear. In this light as well, "the cross, as a locus of divine revelation, is not good news for the powerful, for those who are comfortable with the way things are, or for anyone whose understanding of religion is aligned with power."[31]

Pilate's question to Jesus, "What is truth?" is a question for every interpreter of this Gospel. Through the lens of African American interpretation, what truth will we uphold and defend, especially when we remember that truth for the Gospel of John is not an abstract principle, faith tenet, or belief but the very person of Jesus Christ, "I am the way, and the truth, and the life" (14:6)? Jesus' willingness to speak truth to power is the kind of action that his unfair and unjust trial elicits. When Pilate presents Jesus and says, "Behold the man!" (19:5), "it speaks to Jesus as the one true human who came to restore us all. At the same time, John makes it clear that even as an innocent person condemned to die Jesus is in fact a *person*."[32] This personhood sanctifies the humanity of Black persons.

Holding up an African American approach to the passion narrative of John's Gospel presents significant interpretive possibilities for Jesus' last words from the cross, all unique to the Fourth Gospel. "Woman, behold your son; son, behold your mother" (vv. 26–27) are first words that voice Jesus' own loneliness and abandonment. The first of George Floyd's seven last words as police were killing him were "mama, mama, mama."[33] "When black men were lynched, black women not only suffered the loss of their sons, husbands, brothers, uncles, nephews, and cousins, but also endured public insults and economic hardship as they tried to carry on, to take care of their fatherless children in a patriarchal and racist society in which whites could lynch them or their children with impunity, at the slightest whim or smallest infraction of the southern racial etiquette."[34] From this perspective, the plight of Jesus' mother comes into view. Mary looks upon her son as his life slips away.[35] What kind of insults did the mother of Jesus have to face in the disgrace of Jesus' death? What would a sermon sound like from her viewpoint, the viewpoint of Jesus' Black mother? Every day, Black mothers lose sons to the manifestations of injustice and racism. What is her story once Jesus' body is removed from the cross?

When Jesus cries, "I am thirsty" (v. 28), only then to be offered a drink, we might ask, for what does Jesus thirst? Of course, in the Synoptic accounts, Jesus is given a drink without his request. While "hungering and thirsting for righteousness" is found only in Matthew's Beatitudes, for what might Jesus thirst in the Gospel of John? In John, perhaps Jesus thirsts for a world that might know God's grace upon grace (1:16); a world that might recognize God's love for all persons, even the Samaritan woman whom most would exclude from God's abundance; a world where healing leads to wholeness and restoration to community;[36] a world bent toward emancipation. Perhaps Jesus thirsts for an end to unchecked and oppressive power, an end to racism. Perhaps Jesus' thirst represents an "ontological thirst for life that refuses to let the worst determine our final meaning."[37] When Jesus utters, "It is finished" (19:30), an African American interpretive lens sees that "God's eschatological future . . . would not be defeated by the 'troubles of this world,' no matter how great and painful."[38]

In all three of these last words of Jesus in the Gospel of John, we see Jesus' solidarity with humanity. Solidarity itself is a salvific act to which the songs of Black people give witness. "The spirituals, gospel songs, and hymns focused on how Jesus achieved salvation for the least through his *solidarity* with them even unto death." This solidarity, however, is not just that Jesus suffered and died as humans do. "If the God of Jesus' cross is found among the least, the crucified people of the world, then God is also found among those lynched in American history."[39] Through the lens of African American interpretation, the details of the burial scene (vv. 38–42) in John's Gospel look different as well. "The notice that Jesus' body has been pierced and his bones remain unbroken correlates with the scriptural characteristics of an innocent victim. . . . The absence of sacrificial terms in describing the death of

Jesus suggests that the point of these allusions is Jesus' righteous inno-
cence, not his sacrificial death."[40]

HOMILETICAL IMPLICATIONS

The preacher who commits to an African American approach to biblical interpretation takes an intentional step toward dismantling systemic
racism, especially systemic racism in the church. What will the preacher
say, what will the preacher do, "about the pain and rage that comes
with being Black in this country"?[41] How a preacher speaks about racism, especially the ways in which the church has been complicit in
racism, is both a societal and *theological* concern. It is an ecclesial and
pastoral concern. It is not enough to reject racism and then remain
neutral in the pulpit. "There is no neutrality in the racism struggle."[42]
In the aftermath of the murders of Michael Brown, Trayvon Martin,
Breonna Taylor, Tamir Rice, Freddie Gray, Philando Castile, and
George Floyd,[43] and in the midst of the Black Lives Matter movement,
silence on the part of the preacher communicates complacency on the
part of the church. There can be no "talk of salvation, redemption,
reconciliation, or incarnation" without "discernment of *vocation*. God
chooses not to redeem or reconcile the world without us."[44]

Preaching to confront racism is an essential part of the homiletical landscape in this current time. Preachers need every resource to be
able to navigate the church's response to the sins of systemic racism
and white supremacy. What will the church say? How will the church
contribute to the conversation about addressing the racist policies and
procedures that have allowed racism to survive, even to thrive?

At stake is the very integrity of the church. "The church is a community of truth; church is where we are given the courage, even the responsibility, to say *sin*."[45] How the world sees the response of the church to
racism determines our ecclesial future. The church cannot continue
to blame outside forces for its decline, especially when its preachers
remain silent about the sin of racism. Preachers must be committed
to naming the church's responsibility for its own demise, a demise
due in part to an unwillingness to admit culpability in enabling systemic racism. Silence in the pulpit about racism is a factor that should
lead to questions about the church's relevancy. Not to claim the sin of
racism is to risk the church's integrity, even one's own integrity as a
preacher. "When a preacher dares to tell the truth we've been avoiding,

the preacher pays tribute to the power of Jesus Christ to enable naturally deceitful people to be truthful."[46] We show that our accountability is not to the structures that lead to death, but to the gospel that leads to life.

> Preaching is not primarily about racism or any other sin. Preaching is about the God who, through Jesus Christ, justifies, seeks and saves, loves, forgives, sanctifies, and transforms sinners. We preach about racism in confidence that God wants us to succeed at this task, to free us from our sin against others and to liberate those who are oppressed by the sin and injustice of various domination systems.[47]

We preach against racism not only for that sin to be exposed—in our society, in our churches, in ourselves—but because it is a mandate of the gospel. "Does the Bible have a word to say about the creation of a just society in which Black people can flourish free of oppression?"[48] An African American approach to biblical interpretation insists that at the heart of the gospel is liberation. When we read the biblical texts through this lens, we cannot *not* preach about the sin of racism.

The homiletical silence in not naming the link between the cross and the lynching tree is deafening. Preachers today should, therefore, ask, What prevents us from making this connection? Perhaps we have so theologized the cross, counted on it for the church's survival, that to associate the cross and the lynching tree is too risky. Or perhaps we cannot face our racism and thus remain mute, hoping to avoid having to admit the truth. To correlate the cross and the lynching tree signals solidarity with the African American experience. "Black ministers preached about Jesus' death more than any other theme because they saw in Jesus' suffering and persecution a parallel to their own encounter with slavery, segregation, and the lynching tree."[49] If preachers keep quiet about this dominant theme in Black preaching, how much more then are we mute in the face of systemic and institutional racism?

Preaching about racism also allows for a more comprehensive treatment of sin in our sermons. There is a propensity to focus more on individual sin in our preaching and worship, thereby placing responsibility on persons, as they imagine, to be better people. The resistance to hearing about racism in the pulpit may very well be that preachers have not addressed enough corporate or communal sin—that is, the systemic sin that infiltrates our institutions, including the church. "Something deep within us, widespread among us from generation to generation, inclines us to organize the world as if God were not."[50]

Naming corporate or communal sin is every bit as inherent to the gospel message as coming to terms with our known individual sins. It is to name the human condition of brokenness, not for the sake of blame, but toward recognition, admission, and confession.[51] In this regard, preachers will also widen the definition and imagination of salvation, which tend toward connections to forgiveness.

Preachers must also name the sin of slavery and acknowledge that "in the hands of white slave owners, the Bible was a tool of oppression."[52] How will we preachers address the passages about slavery in the Bible? Is the preacher aware of those passages, and are they redeemable in any way?[53] We can condemn these passages outright, but condemnation without intentions toward reparations will ring hollow. And condemnation is not the same as naming the Black experience of these passages. "The enslaved people read (or heard) in the biblical texts about a God who delighted in liberation, and this gave them hope. It was not that the slave passages didn't exist; they simply couldn't be used to undo the testimony of the exodus."[54]

The preacher who brings an African American perspective to interpreting Scripture toward preaching also names the sin of white supremacy.[55] This is a challenging homiletical reality because it means self-interrogation on the part of the church, the preacher, and each member of the congregation. It means admitting the ways in which we have perpetuated the idea of white supremacy, in thought, word, and deed, or in what we have not done. If Will Willimon is right, that "the defeat of white supremacy calls for more robust theologizing,"[56] then the church and its preachers are called to engage in theological discourse and proclamation that demonstrates active theological construction. Preaching demands constant theological reconstruction and renewal, as the Word of God gets reincarnated in the lives of God's people in our constantly changing contexts. This means also a commitment to knowing as intimately as possible the Black struggle in the United States. It is to be vigilant in our human tendency to assume that we can *will* ourselves to be better than what past human behavior has divulged. All too frequently, this kind of social justice preaching devolves into a moralistic homiletic that "overlooks how structural, systemic principalities and powers have us under their sway."[57]

When a white person engages an African American approach to preaching, it is essential to have an awareness of the goal or purpose, as well as the four essentials of the Black sermon: God, Scripture, the preacher, Black lived experience.[58] Often the hoped-for result is a collective move toward reconciliation, specifically interpersonal reconciliation, but rarely an awareness of necessity for communal or corporate reconciliation. That is, there is a call for reconciliation, yet "without recognition of power arrangements" and "without focus on systemic and structural reconciliation or justice." To preach reconciliation "presumes there was a time when we were in a right relationship and implies that we work toward reconciliation from an equal footing."[59] A primary goal of an African American approach to biblical interpretation and to preaching is to "empower people who claim to follow [Jesus] to take a stand against white supremacy and every kind of injustice."[60]

An African American hermeneutic calls attention to a glaring misinterpretation of Scripture on the part of many Christians—to view ourselves as the insiders, when in fact, "we were the Gentiles on the margins," included later into God's covenant with Israel.[61] We do not preach about racism because we are concerned about resistance and rejection. We are worried about numbers and membership. And yet, we preachers need to remember that the resistance is not about us and what we say but about being faced with the truth of how we participate in systems, known and unknown, that perpetuate racism. The truth is never easy to hear, especially when we come up against a truth about ourselves over which we thought we had control.

This kind of truth telling calls for a prophetic stance on the part of the preacher, but we cannot forget that "the first prophetic move is tears."[62] If we bifurcate our prophetic voice from our pastoral heart, we abandon true prophetic preaching. The prophets of the Old Testament indeed spoke the truth to God's people, but that truth was spoken from love—God's love for God's people. While the visions of the prophets were often difficult words to hear, some of the most beautiful passages of Scripture are found in the prophetic books. The prophetic books were first and foremost historical books, not predictive writings. The prophets accompanied God's people, casting visions of the future only insofar as the past and present situation could determine. Today's prophetic preachers committed to dismantling racism do the same—we accompany God's people toward a right relationship with God. Will our sermons speak out against injustice? What history of our congregations, our communities, our nation, and our world is being told in our sermons? What theology is being communicated when there is silence about the African American experience?

FURTHER RESOURCES FOR PREACHING

Helsel, Carolyn. *Preaching about Racism: A Guide for Faith Leaders*. St. Louis: Chalice Press, 2018.

LaRue, Cleophus J. *The Heart of Black Preaching*. Louisville, KY: Westminster John Knox Press, 2000.

Thomas, Frank. *Introduction to the Practice of African American Preaching*. Nashville: Abingdon, 2016.

Valle-Ruiz, Lis, and Andrew Wymer, eds. *Unmasking White Preaching: Racial Hegemony, Resistance, and Possibilities in Homiletics*. Lanham, MD: Lexington Books, 2022.

5

Latinx and Asian American Interpretation

INTRODUCTION

Latinx[1] and Asian American biblical interpretation have been grouped in this chapter because they share the similar concerns of peoples straddling dual identities. They exist with a kind of hybrid citizenship, with one foot in the culture of their ancestry and the other in American society.[2] Latinx and Asian American biblical interpretation are also convened together to underscore the problems with terminology. The categories Latinx, Latino/a, and Asian function as umbrella terms that exist primarily for the convenience of white persons. Lost in these designations is the diversity they hold and, therefore, the diversity in approaches to reading and interpreting the Bible. It is beyond the scope of this book to summarize the subsets of representation that both "Latinx" and "Asian American" signify. How does one, for example, define the term "Asian"? "Asian can include everyone in Asia, specific culture groups, or a specific culture group within a specific location."[3] A specific focus on a Korean interpretation of a passage in the Bible, for example, is not likely transferable for the preacher—nor should it be. The fact that we cannot bring a specific Mexican, South American (and its many representations), Indian, Japanese, and so forth, lens to interpreting the Bible is the point of a focus on these approaches. Specifically for the white reader, it is virtually impossible. The strategy employed here will identify larger themes and yet acknowledge this radically simplified approach. Limitations of the capacity for nuance must be consistently noted by the reader and the preacher.

General themes found in common between Latinx and Asian American biblical interpretation might include—but this certainly does not exhaust the possibilities—displacement, migration, minoritization, and marginalization. Such themes are observably prominent in the Bible, even from its beginning, Genesis's opening myth of Adam and Eve being displaced from Eden. The Abrahamic narrative is one of migration. The Letters of Paul speak to minoritized communities trying to exist within the Roman Empire and the imperial cult. Jesus encounters one marginalized person after another, ostracized for reasons of sickness and status. Connecting the contextual experiences of Latinx and Asian American persons and the people and characters of the Bible is but one way for the preacher to demonstrate how biblical themes can point to timeless truths about the human condition. The challenge with the themes of displacement, migration, minoritization, and marginalization is to avoid reductionism in our preaching, particularly when preaching from and to the majority and the privileged. Feeling left out is not the same as systemic and institutional marginalization. Having to move from one's country to another is not the same as the plight of immigrants.

SUMMARY OF THE APPROACHES

Latinx and Asian American approaches are extraordinarily diverse, which is true for any perspective that is rooted in contextual or ideological viewpoints. Francisco Lozado Jr. warns against any kind of "master narrative" and assumption "that a Puerto Rican, Mexican American, Cuban American, Dominican, Salvadoran, Guatemalan, or Bolivian (to name a few) reading is representative of the views of the entire Latino/a community in the United States."[4] This means that a primary issue for Latinx interpretation is the question of identity. Lai Ling Elizabeth Ngan writes, "The term 'Asian American' is used to classify an extremely ethnically diverse group of people. It signifies persons of Asian heritage who identify themselves as Americans. Whether they are of the first or fourth generation in the United States, they have settled and negotiated their way into the dominant American culture."[5] What follows is a presentation of each approach separately, followed by a concluding discussion of the shared theme of dual citizenship as a lens for interpreting the Bible.

With Latinx approaches to biblical interpretation, the challenge is to represent the diversity of this perspective but at the same time be able "to identify common threads and shared experiences."[6] M. Daniel Carroll R. identifies one shared experience as "longtime social marginalization and discrimination."[7] While Latino/a approaches are difficult to define, "what all Latino/a groups do seem to have in common is the perception by 'non-Latino/as' that they are 'Others' in the United States."[8] Fernando F. Segovia suggests that Latinx interpretation "subscribes to the basic tenets of liberation theology."[9] There can be no uniform strategies or taxonomies, and yet when interpreting the Bible, "Latinos/as find meaning for life, analogous experiences of displaced minority peoples, wrestling with hybrid identities, compassionate legislation for the outside, and the assurance of God's presence in their troubles."[10] There is the desire in Latinx interpretation "to provide hope in *lo cotidiano* (the experience of daily life) and to give diaspora existence significance with God and before others." The Bible itself is a compendium of diaspora experiences, and "human history is the history of migration."[11] Justo L. González suggests five lenses integral for Latinx interpretation: marginality, poverty, *mestizaje* and *mulatez* (mixed race combinations[12]), exiles and aliens, and solidarity.[13] Latinx interpretation will seek to show the similarities between the Latinx experience "and the life and ministry of Jesus, a Jew from the cultural and political backwater of Galilee. This otherness was fundamental to Jesus' identification with the marginalized and his challenge to the religious authorities in Jerusalem."[14]

Eric Barreto describes the benefits of Latinx interpretation as a way to engage fully "with the complexities of race and ethnicity" in the Bible so that the contingency of "ethnic particularity" does not "tear us apart" but will "bring us together."[15] One of the theological developments in early Christianity was to emphasize that union in the body of Christ eliminates all differences. Drawing on Paul's declamation in Galatians 3:28, "There is no longer Jew or Greek, there is no longer slave or free, there is no longer male and female; for all of you are one in Christ Jesus," Christianity is thus portrayed as a radically inclusive movement, being united in Christ, and therefore "all of you are one" means all are the same. In Latino/a biblical hermeneutic and preaching, Barreto finds an important critique of this tendency.

> These depictions emerge from a clearly positive desire to see the end of the ethnic and racial strife that pervades our world and our shared histories. However, by denying the continued importance of racial and ethnic differences among early Christians, such reconstructions advocate an inaccurate portrayal with significant impact today. In our hope to make racism a relic of the past, we may strive too quickly and move too easily into a mode of forgetfulness or denial. Unfortunately, when we are all made the same, too often those in power get to dictate the rules of unity. Homogeneity is imagined under the terms of the majority. Unity then consists of becoming more like the powerful and numerous rather than an equitable negotiation in the midst of great diversity. By denying the reality of difference, we may end up only exacerbating the problem of prejudice. By denying that the earliest Christians and Scripture embraced difference in deep and powerful ways, we tell incorrectly the story of faith.[16]

For Barreto, "ethnic identity is not an obstacle to Christian theology and God's aims of liberation but inherent to the work of God through God's diverse people. The New Testament does not project a world in which God effaces our differences but a world in which God invites all God's people to live into the complexities, promises, and perils of our differences."[17]

Asian American biblical interpretation posits similar yet distinctive themes. Within the Asian American field of study, there is neither a single approach or method nor little agreement, but "a discourse that acknowledges both the multicultural and trans-generational infrastructure of Asian America and the social and political dynamics at play in the Asian American experience."[18] The term itself is problematic. As Frank M. Yamada notes, "It is limited in its descriptive value. To put all Americans of Asian background into one racial grouping does not do justice to the particularities among the different groups. The racial category of Asian American covers people from many different nationalities—Japanese, Chinese, Korean, Filipino, Vietnamese, Indian, etc."[19] Or, as K. K. Yeo writes, "In Asia, difference surpasses commonality, hybridity takes the place of singularity, and multiplicity overshadows uniformity."[20] In general, Asian American interpretation "wrestles with the problem of the liminal and marginalized existence in the critical context of empire and colonial hegemony" navigating "contexts of dislocation, migration, and displacement"[21] and the complexities of identity, immigration, "multiple cultural allegiances, marginalization vis-à-vis mainstream society, historical exclusion."[22]

A distinctive feature of Asian American biblical interpretation is the way in which cultural metaphors are adapted to engage theological concepts and biblical interpretation. For example, "the ancient Chinese cosmology of 'yin-yang' (which literally means a "shaded area" and a "brightly lit area" that are in constant flux) is often reappropriated by Asian scholars to speak of the marginality and in-betweenness of theological method (including biblical interpretation)."[23]

For the sake of summary, Andrew Yueking Lee outlines six issues that shape Asian American interpretation of the Bible: (1) "Marginality and liminality," because "an Asian American culturally lives between the worlds of Asia and America, fully belonging to neither." (2) "Inclusiveness," because the "ambiguity of living in two worlds and making sense out of each of them means that life is filled with tension." (3) "Suffering and sacrifice," because of the "suffering and pain as a result of racism in the United States." (4) "Pilgrimage versus materialism," because Asian Americans "will never be able to enter fully into American society the way that a European immigrant can." (5) "Corporate versus individual thinking," because "biblical passages that address the element of life together, especially in regard to the family, would be in harmony with traditional Asian teaching." (6) "Law versus grace," because of the emphasis in Asian culture on meeting expectations.[24]

As diverse as these two approaches are, a common thread for both Latinx and Asian American biblical interpretation is the feeling of having one foot in one world and the other foot in another. As Rubén R. Dupertuis notes, a "sense of belonging to more than one world at once is easily one of the core elements of Latino/a experiences."[25] Jacqueline M. Hidalgo argues that critical for Latino/a identity in the United States is this sense of being "neither Latin American nor United Statesan, but caught in some world between."[26] The same phenomenon describes the experience of "Asian American Christians living in, and *in-between*, two worlds (i.e., Asia and America). Globalization subjects them to rapid change and often threatens their immigrant identity of *double-rootedness*, so they are therefore unable to live fully in either place."[27] Frank Yamada describes Asian American theology as existing in a kind of in-betweenness, "between the cultures of their Asian ancestry and the dominant American society."[28]

SAMPLE TEXT: JOHN 17

Latinx and Asian American biblical interpretation both offer a number of themes through which to view the Bible, several of which will be discussed in more detail in the "Homiletical Implications" section below. For this discussion of a sample text, the lens will be the shared experience in both communities of betwixt and betweenness, how both communities have a sense of dual citizenship.[29] They feel caught between two worlds, with "a sense of belonging and yet not belonging."[30] Jacqueline M. Hidalgo describes this for the Latinx community as having to "navigate experiences of (no) placement," being forced to consider, "How do boundaries of identity and (un) belonging get drawn? Why do these boundaries get drawn, what is it at stake in their drawing, and how are texts deployed in order to mark and cross borders?"[31] Cristina Garcia-Alfonso explains this as living in "two dwelling places," not living "fully in either . . . but in the center."[32] This straddling of two worlds also brings about a sense of being "othered." In the case of Latinx criticism, "Since we have to construct our world in light of an identity of otherness, we understand the plight of the first Christians as meaning-makers and world-constructors in light of the Christ event."[33]

Bringing this lens to the Gospel of John, how might the identity of a follower of Christ be described similarly? How do the disciples of Jesus also find themselves in an in-between kind of existence? How do we?

Widely known as the High Priestly Prayer, chapter 17 in the Gospel of John concludes the Farewell Discourse (chaps. 13–17), Jesus' final words to his disciples before his arrest, trial, and crucifixion.[34] The longest of any of Jesus' prayers in the Gospel accounts, the High Priestly Prayer unfolds in three sections with three distinct emphases. In 17:1–5, Jesus prays to the Father for himself. In verses 6–19, the focus shifts to his current disciples. The last portion of the prayer turns to disciples yet to be who will become believers because of the witness of the disciples. Jesus' final prayer in John is not at the scene of his arrest, as it is in Matthew 26:36–46, Mark 14:32–42, and Luke 22:39–46. Instead, it occurs while Jesus and his disciples are still together in the room where Jesus washes the disciples' feet and where they share a meal; where Judas betrays Jesus and where Peter's denial is foretold; and where Jesus says his parting words to the disciples. It is after the prayer that Jesus and his disciples leave the room, cross the Kidron Valley (the valley between the Mount of Olives and the eastern entrance into Jerusalem), and enter a garden, presumably somewhere on the Mount of Olives, outside of which Jesus will be arrested (John 18:1–11).

A unique feature of Jesus' final prayer in John is that the disciples overhear every word Jesus speaks. Unlike the Synoptic Gospels, in which Jesus goes off alone to pray, leaving the disciples, who then promptly fall asleep, John's narrative has the disciples able to hear Jesus praying for himself, for them, and for the believers who will be theirs to find. Situated within the Farewell Discourse, the prayer addresses the crisis to which Jesus' words speak—his departure. The disciples will be left without Jesus' presence because the incarnation, as it must, will come to an end with Jesus' crucifixion. However, they are not left "orphaned" (14:18) because Jesus will send his followers another Paraclete to be with them forever (v. 16).[35] With the promise of the Paraclete who will accompany the disciples in this world, the Farewell Discourse closes with Jesus' High Priestly Prayer.

The disciples need to hear the promise of the Paraclete because Jesus is clear in the prayer that in leaving his disciples, he is also leaving them in the world that hates them.

> I have given them your word, and the world has hated them because they do not belong to the world, just as I do not belong to the world. I am not asking you to take them out of the world, but I ask you to protect them from the evil one. They do not belong to the world, just as I do not belong to the world. Sanctify them in the truth; your word is truth. As you have sent me into the world, so I have sent them into the world. And for their sakes I sanctify myself, so that they also may be sanctified in truth. (17:14–19)

The world is a prominent character in the Gospel of John. It is the object of God's love, "For God so loved the world that he gave his only Son, so that everyone who believes in him may not perish but may have eternal life" (3:16), but it rejects God's love, "He was in the world, and the world came into being through him; yet the world did not know him" (1:10). The term *kosmos* appears more than seventy times in the Fourth Gospel and eighteen times in chapter 17 alone. Once the world chooses Barabbas over Jesus—"After [Pilate] had said this, he went out to the Jews again and told them, 'I find no case against him. But you have a custom that I release someone for you at the Passover. Do you want me to release for you the King of the Jews?' They shouted in reply, 'Not this man, but Barabbas!' Now Barabbas was a bandit" (18:38–40)—"world" does not appear again in the narrative until the conclusion to the Gospel, "But there are also many other things that Jesus did; if every one of them were written down, I suppose that the world itself could not contain the books that would be written" (21:25). The last occurrence of "world" before Jesus' crucifixion is during the trial before Pilate, "Jesus answered, 'You say that I am a king. For this I was born, and for this I came into the world, to testify to the truth. Everyone who belongs to the truth listens to my voice'" (18:37). With the crucifixion, and thus the resurrection and ascension, Jesus is no longer in the world. The world then disappears from the narrative.

In the history of Johannine scholarship, John's use of the term "world" is often assumed to be positing a radical exclusivity. This dualism of us and them, however, has to be situated within the wider discussion of the intended audience for John's Gospel. Scholarly consensus holds that the community to which John was writing had experienced some kind of excommunication for their belief in Jesus as the Messiah, signaled by the term *aposynagōgos* (put out of the synagogue; 9:22;-12:42; 16:2).

Throughout the Gospel, there are allusions to and statements of being in this world and not of this world. "He said to them, 'You are from below, I am from above; you are of this world, I am not of this world'" (8:23). The true light comes into the world (1:9; 3:19; 12:46–47), but "people loved darkness rather than light" (3:19). Jesus is seen as "the prophet who is to come into the world" (6:14). The world hates Jesus: "The world cannot hate you, but it hates me because I testify against it that its works are evil" (7:7). Jesus must leave this world to return to the Father: "Now before the festival of the Passover, Jesus knew that his hour had come to depart from this world and go to the Father. Having loved his own who were in the world, he loved them to the end" (13:1). Jesus' kingdom is not of this world (18:36). The world appears with the most frequency in the Farewell Discourse. It is in this narrative portion of the Gospel that Jesus shares he is leaving this world and leaving the disciples in this world.[36] The disciples must stay in this world for the sake of God's love for the world. "I have other sheep that do not belong to this fold. I must bring them also, and they will listen to my voice. So there will be one flock, one shepherd" (10:16). Jesus will send the disciples into the world with the presence and promise of the Holy Spirit. "Jesus said to them again, 'Peace be with you. As the Father has sent me, so I send you.' When he had said this, he breathed on them and said to them, 'Receive the Holy Spirit'" (20:21–22). Jesus will commission Peter to feed Jesus' sheep, thus remaining in the world (21:15–19).

The repetition of "world" in the High Priestly Prayer is striking.[37] All of what has been said about the world thus far in the Gospel is brought forward to Jesus' prayer to the Father. "And now I am no longer in the world, but they are in the world, and I am coming to you. Holy Father, protect them in your name that you have given me, so that they may be one, as we are one" (17:11). The two worlds remain but are now caught up in the unity of the Father, Jesus, the Spirit, and the believer, a promise that abstains from explanation. The disciples find themselves caught between two worlds. It is a challenging existence, to be sure, but a necessary one when worlds have collided in the incarnation.

This dual citizenship of the disciples is better understood considering Latinx and Asian American biblical interpretation. Neither world is left behind in favor of the other, nor should that be an expectation. Identity is lodged in both, just as was true for Jesus. Attempts to dislodge one from the other become moot by the language of unity in the High Priestly Prayer. While the two worlds still maintain separate existences, in the incarnation, crucifixion, resurrection, and ascension, mysteriously and transcendently, these worlds are now one. Attempts to locate these worlds on a linear plane are faulty in the theological claim that the infinite has become finite; the atemporal has entered time; the preexistent Word has become flesh.

The realities of being between two worlds, or existing in two worlds, are also brought to light through the subtheme of migration. Gilberto A. Ruiz observes that John "features the most border-crossings by Jesus," in Galilee, Samaria, and Judea.[38] Geographically, this is true in that John has Jesus traveling back and forth between Galilee and Judea/Jerusalem recurrently, unlike the Synoptic Gospels, which place Jesus in Jerusalem only once. Theologically, however, "the most important border-crossing that takes place in the Fourth Gospel is cosmic."[39] Jesus leaves this world and returns to the Father, which completes the full circle of his ministry embodied in the incarnation, crucifixion, resurrection, and ascension. Jesus ascends to the Father as the one who descended, the Son of Man (1:51). And yet, because Jesus came into this world, the separation of worlds is complexified. Through the Latinx and Asian American interpretive lens of being betwixt and between two worlds, the two-worlds existence experienced by Jesus' disciples resists spiritualization. The Latinx and Asian American reality highlights the competing identities and loyalties, the struggle narrated in

John's Gospel and a common challenge for Christian discipleship today. The dual worlds posited by John because of Jesus represent both of Jesus' identities, neither of which can be let go for the other. Jesus knows this tension as fully human and fully divine. "He crosses the divide between the heavenly realm and the earthly, and it is through this migratory incarnation that salvation is offered to the world. . . . John presents a 'migration-centered' Christology."[40]

HOMILETICAL IMPLICATIONS

Tending to Latinx and Asian American perspectives for biblical interpretation has several key homiletical implications. As discussed above, preaching on the dual citizenship of discipleship can easily devolve into sentimentalization, where being in this world and not of this world is simply a metaphor for the challenges of obedience to God. The betwixt and between of the Latinx and Asian American existence is not symbolic but lived experience. As believers, navigating our allegiance to God's reign is real. From the perspective of Latinx and Asian American interpretation, loyalty is enfleshed. Latinx and Asian American interpretation also guards against a kind of apocalypticism prominent in much of Christianity, insisting that this world matters little because of our future eternal life with God.

Being the "Others" or "othered" in the United States as noted above, the Latinx interpretive perspective helps contemporary Christians remember that they were once the "othered." Christians today forget that we were once the minority, the "Others," or the Gentiles, to use a New Testament term. Christians are used to existing in a mainstreamed Christianity and in religious systems that continue to exist because of privilege. A Latinx perspective calls attention to the truth of the origins of Christianity and our propensity to "other," especially in our approaches to reading the Bible. Christian believers are thus reminded of their "otherness" even in how the well-meaning faithful see themselves as the insiders, the chosen. "By foregrounding the Latino/a experience, this approach destabilizes not only the myth that the United States is a homogeneous, monolingual, or monocultural country, but also the field of biblical studies and the paradigms of privileged cultures. Said another way, it challenges the notion that the production of knowledge emanates from one particular economic and socio-educational exclusive community."[41] At the same time, "the Bible can raise the majority culture's awareness of the strangers in their midst."[42]

Latinx interpretation also aids in preaching about migration.[43] As the United States is a country full of migrants, "migration remains a topic of political controversy and subaltern urgency in the United States" but is also "a global problem" caused by "war, politics, economics, and human-caused climate change."[44] The Latinx experience affords the preacher with more nuanced awareness of and ability to talk about the theme of migration in biblical texts; how migration, exile, and diaspora have influenced Jewish and Christian Scripture; and how "migration, diaspora, and hybridity were foundational to the start and growth of the Christian church."[45] With a Latinx interpretative perspective, we are better able to recognize how "the Christian Bible is a collection of texts of and about migration."[46] An intentional sermon on migration in a biblical passage can be a starting point or occasion for communal conversations around migration. "We might best understand biblical texts as sites where people have wrestled with different responses to migration and its experiences."[47] As a result, migration is not then a problem to fix or eradicate but a situation endemic to the human condition. "A migrant perspective, in other words, can help all Christians better understand their true identity" as "strangers in a strange land."[48]

Attention to Asian American biblical interpretation in preaching helps the preacher realize that "a recurring issue among minority communities is a sense of inferiority." Where in our preaching do we speak of the "value of the outsider" and the "worth of the stranger"?[49] When there are texts that feature this dynamic, do we make connections to minoritized persons? In doing so, preachers can then also address in the pulpit hate and hate crimes directed at Asian Americans, especially in the wake of the COVID-19 pandemic. It is human nature to cast blame when there is discomfort, but the derogatory and hateful attributions blaming Asian Americans for the pandemic constitute outright discrimination. That the prejudice and bias were perpetrated by the sitting president of the United States, calling the coronavirus the "China flu," "Chinese virus," and "Kung flu," demands words from the pulpit that denounce such racism. An Asian American approach to interpreting the Bible certainly does not need validation from the pulpit, but bringing the perspective into the sermon in some way communicates worth.

Tending to Latino/a and Asian American interpretation provides opportunity for doing faith formation, especially with a focus on identity and what forms identity. Faith formation is central to ministry, happening not only in programmatic offerings such as Sunday school, adult forums, and confirmation, but also by means of the sermon. Imagining the sermon as a faith formation event and process means that the sermon is never just about the meaning of a biblical passage in this place and time, for these people and this purpose, but it also shapes theological imagination and nurtures Christian identity. Faith and identity formation do not occur in a bubble. We are not Christians in one setting and then identify as German, for example, separately. The embodiment of faith's principles and faith's allegiances happens in daily life. As a result, preachers need to consider how faith formation is an integral part of identity formation. Faith, belief structures, and religious life are shaped by other aspects of identity formation. Recognizing the intersectionality of faith and identity formation is critical for an integrated Christian life in which faith is not just what happens on Sunday. Conversation around identity formation might then help people realize the connectedness between belief and expression of identity. Were the church to be a place for that conversation, some of the siloism of religious debate might ebb. Identity as a complex reality then becomes a fundamental subject of dialogue in our churches.

FURTHER RESOURCES FOR PREACHING

González, Justo L., and Pablo A. Jiménez. *Púlpito: An Introduction to Hispanic Preaching*. Nashville: Abingdon Press, 2005.

Kim, Eunjoo Mary. *Preaching the Presence of God: A Homiletic from an Asian American Perspective*. Valley Forge, PA: Judson, 1999.

6

Queer Interpretation

INTRODUCTION

Queer theory "can be traced to the prominent gay-rights movement of the late 1960s and early 1970s."[1] Queer biblical interpretation is a more recent focus in biblical scholarship because queer theology has a short history in theological discourse.[2]

By way of introduction to the approach, a glossary of terms is necessary. The first term to consider is *queer*. Patrick S. Cheng identifies three meanings for the word "queer": first, as "an umbrella term; second, as transgressive action; and third, as erasing boundaries."[3] Pamela R. Lightsey writes, "Queer is ambiguous not simply because it is being reclaimed in new ways but because it proposes that while sexuality is real, it should not be construed as necessarily taking one permanent form. To identify as queer is to assert a type of fluidity in life, particularly sexuality. In fact, the fluidity of sexuality is the freedom of possibility, the possibility to be sexually attracted in multifarious ways."[4] Within biblical interpretation, the term "has come to denote a hermeneutical position similar to other late-twentieth-century theories such as third-wave feminism and postcolonialism, all of which denaturalize or de-essentialize formerly stable identities such as homosexuality, heterosexuality, race, nationality, woman, and man."[5]

Historically, the term "queer" holds a derogatory connotation, only recently recovered by scholars who identify as LGBTQIA+ (lesbian, gay, bisexual, transgender, queer, intersex, asexual, questioning). "The fact that queer is now a politically acceptable term is due to the rigorous work of LGBT activists against political and police oppression."[6] As an umbrella term, queer is a synonym for LGBTQIA+ persons. It functions as a "collective term to describe people with marginalized sexualities (lesbian, gay, or bisexual) as well as with marginalized gender identities (transgender) or genitalia (intersex)."[7]

It is critical in queer theory to note the difference between sexuality and gender identity. Sexuality can be understood as "emotional and physical attraction"[8] regardless of the gender of the object of that attraction. Gender identity "refers to the ways in which people self-identify with respect to their genders ('female' or 'male'), regardless of the sex that they were assigned at birth."[9] The distinction between sexuality and gender identity is a vital component in queer studies, especially when these distinctions are blurred in the interpretation of the Bible and "homosexuality."

Queer can also be understood as transgressive action; that is, it "embraces all that is transgressive or opposed to society norms, particularly with respect to sexuality and gender identity."[10] This second definition has a focus on action; it is better understood as a verb. Therefore, "to 'queer' something is to engage with a methodology that challenges and disrupts the status quo."[11]

The third meaning of queer connects with queer theory that became a focus of inquiry in academics in the 1990s. It is the intent of queer theory to complexify "queerness," especially as sexuality and gender identity are socially constructed. Sexuality as connected to one's identity was not a social reality until the term "homosexuality" was introduced, where "a person's *identity* was defined or categorized in terms of the gender of her or his preferred sexual partner(s)."[12] Sexuality was then directly linked to *being* rather than behavior. Recent studies in queer theory have argued against the binaries of so-called normative sexuality, either homosexuality or heterosexuality, when bisexuality, for example, proves the fluidity of sexuality; sexuality is a spectrum. Gender identity is also a social construct based on social norms of gender expression. Gender is a performative act,[13] and, like sexuality, resists binaries of female and male. Gender expression as a manifestation of gender identity is not inherent to one's stated biological sex. To summarize, the third meaning of queer as a boundary-erasing methodology challenges social norms with regard to the fixed binaries of sexuality and gender.

Bringing queer theory to queer theology, Cheng offers three defini-tions of what queer theology might include. "First, queer theology is LGBT people 'talking about God.' Second, queer theology is 'talking about God' in a self-consciously transgressive manner, especially in terms of challenging societal norms about sexuality and gender. Third, queer theology is 'talk about God' that challenges and deconstructs the natural binary categories of sexual and gender identity."[14]

Like any theological approach, queer theology wrestles with at least four sources for theological reflection: Scripture, reason, tradi-tion, and experience.[15] This is particularly helpful for the preacher to remember—how we think theologically is never based on the Bible alone but reflects the interface of these sources, with every interpretive move a favoring of one over the other three. Furthermore, denom-inations themselves tend to uphold one source over the other, giv-ing it more weight in its theological emphases and ecclesiological constructs.

Some additional definitions might help the preacher. *Transgender* people "identify with a gender that is different from their assigned sex at birth."[16] Transgender "identification is possible regardless of whether or not one transitions socially or medically."[17] *Cisgender* means the opposite: people who do identify with the gender they were assigned at birth. *Gender-neutral, gender-queer,* and *gender-nonbinary* persons choose not to identify with either gender.[18] In summary, "Queer theory is not just for or about so-called homosexuals. It is critical theory con-cerned principally with cultural deployments of power through social constructions of sexuality and gender."[19]

SUMMARY OF THE APPROACH

Like the approaches presented in the previous chapters, a queer approach to Scripture is grounded in the queer experience and is as var-ied as the contexts of the interpreters. At the same time, queer theology "specifically addresses the complexities of gender identities in the Bible and in our world. And it demonstrates over and over again that gender is rendered by performance, that there is no unique and essential way of being a man or a woman, heterosexual, homosexual, bisexual, or transgender. There exists no objective, epistemological, and monolithic construct for sexual identities. They are simply too vast, too complex, and too fluid."[20]

A first identifying claim of queer theology related to queer biblical interpretation is the extent to which Christian theology itself "is fundamentally a queer enterprise."[21] That is, in the coming of Jesus Christ, the binaries on which we construct our world get contested and finally erode. The "incarnation, life, death, resurrection, ascension, and second coming of Jesus Christ . . . are events that turn upside down our traditional understanding of life and death, divine and human, center and margins, beginnings and endings, infinite and finite, and punishment and forgiveness."[22]

Another important aspect of queer theology, particularly for understanding a queer approach to Scripture, is the doctrine of revelation. Inherent to God is revelation, God's own "coming out" so as to be in relationship with God's people, revealing God's "radical love"[23] for all.

While a number of theological concepts get reworked and recast from a queer theoretical perspective, the definition of sin surfaces as a crucial topic for queer theology because, historically, to be queer is to be labeled sinful or living in sin. Cheng argues that for LGBT persons, sin is best understood as the "rejection of God's radical love," which is "a love so extreme that it dissolves existing boundaries."[24] If radical love is this boundary-breaking, binary-dissolving kind of love, then sin is essentialism or the reinforcement of society's dichotomies. Jesus Christ himself embodied radical love by dissolving the boundary between human and divine.

With attention to sex, gender, flesh, and bodies, a queer perspective on Scripture is aware of the real bodies in the text. "Queer hermeneutics, queer ways of interpreting and knowing . . . search for the bodies in which God is to be found."[25] A focus on the body aligns with the Christian doctrine of the incarnation. Queer hermeneutics calls essential Christian claims to task, especially just how central the doctrine of the incarnation is to our theology and our preaching, where the incarnation is "the making holy of the body." Christianity "is a story about God's incarnation . . . a story in which each person is the object of God's care, attention, and love."[26] Queer theology asks: Is that something we really believe? As Linn Marie Tonstad notes, "Christianity is a story of God's presence among the dissolute, and God's own dissolution (on the cross)."[27] If we are serious about these claims, then attention to this radical commitment to humanity, to the body, should be far more present in our sermons. The separations and binaries that make up our social order were fundamentally "ruptured by a Christ who gave his life for all, but most particularly, the despised."[28]

Ken Stone outlines the following general characteristics of queer criticism:[29]

1. "Queer criticism calls attention to sexual practice and gender . . . as key sites for the interpretation of cultural, social, and textual meanings and practices."
2. "Queer criticism emphasizes the fact that meanings and practices associated with sex, gender, and kinship vary significantly across cultures and histories, or even within a single culture."
3. Queer approaches are "suspicious of organizing sexual and gender meanings too rigidly around stable binary oppositions such as male and female, masculine and feminine, or heterosexual and homosexual. Instead, queer criticism emphasizes the fluidity and unpredictability of gender, sexual desire, and sexual practice, as well as the instability of the binary oppositions that are thought to structure them."
4. Queer perspectives analyze critically "heteronormativity."
5. "Queer criticism focuses on cultural phenomena, practices, and individuals that do not conform to heteronormative ideals."
6. Queer perspectives explore how "norms and practices for gender, sex, and kinship are intertwined with other sorts of norms and practices."

Like feminist approaches, a queer perspective can also bring a "revisionist approach"[30] to discover more about possible same-sex relationships in Scripture such as those between Jonathan and David, Ruth and Naomi, and Jesus and the Beloved Disciple.

SAMPLE TEXTS

In queer biblical interpretation, there are many resonances with the theological world of the Gospel of John. Richard E. Goss writes, "By far, John is the queerest of all the Gospels."[31] When it comes to preaching John from a viewpoint of queer experience, we will consider several textual features and moments in the Gospel.

If "central to John's Gospel is the theme of God's coming out in Jesus"[32] in that God is revealing God's true self, how much more is this the case for the characters in the narrative whom Jesus encounters? From a queer perspective, God's coming out in Jesus is foundational when it comes to interpreting the Gospel of John. In their encounters with Jesus, characters realize "the grace of their true selves."[33] In God's coming out through Jesus in John, queer interpreters view their own coming out experiences as experiences of simultaneous grace and rejection. The rejection of Jesus by the world and the rejection of the Johannine community for believing in Jesus signifies this similar situation for queer folks. In coming out, testifying to their true selves, queer persons face expulsion, just as the members of the Johannine community were expelled from their synagogue and community.

The sectarianism of John's Gospel reflects the experiences of queer Christians, as "many could not accept the coming out of the Word because it was too scandalous, too embodied, and too gracious."[34] The oft-repeated statements of the world's rejection, both of Jesus and of his disciples, are representative of the experience of queer Christians. Even Jesus' own did not accept him (John 1:11).[35] Queer interpretation notes that LGBTQIA+ persons face equal religious hostility. For queer theology, Jesus' Farewell Discourse is "addressed to queer Christians, living in a hostile world. Queer Christians have been expelled from their churches because of their same-sex love."[36]

The prologue to John's Gospel (vv. 1–18) orients the narrative toward this theme of coming out with emphasis on the presence of the light. "The light is revealed but rejected."[37] Recognizing this coming out as a "divine invitation" suggests God's desire for us "to leave behind old patterns and to live authentic lives."[38] Even the enfleshed Word is a point of association for queer Christians as a gender-fluid reality, the mutability of divine wisdom in Jesus, the man. The imagery of being born children of God—"But to all who received him, who believed in his name, he gave power to become children of God, who were born, not of blood or of the will of the flesh or of the will of man, but of God" (vv. 12–13)—becomes a significant touch point for queer theology. Coming out is like being born again.[39] In this regard, "coming out is never a one-time event, nor is it ultimately private. The coming out process lasts a lifetime because we live in a world in which heterosexism is presumed. Because gay and lesbian people have no distinguishing external features, such as skin color, it is easy for us to 'pass' as heterosexuals; therefore, we find ourselves in situations in which we are constantly making decisions about coming out."[40]

Through the lens of a queer perspective, there can be no remaining in the closet. Nicodemus, for example, becomes the "archetypal closeted Christian."[41] Even in the end, Nicodemus pairs up with the closeted disciple, Joseph of Arimathea, to bury Jesus' body in secret, "afraid of the communal consequences in making a decision to come out as a follower of Jesus."[42] This fear of the consequences of coming out is a prominent theme throughout the Gospel of John. The parents of the man born blind, for example, must navigate between the outing of their son and the reaction from the religious authorities (9:18–23). "How often have parents been forced to choose between their children who come out and their church with its narrow ethical definitions and rituals of exclusion and coercion!"[43]

The raising of Lazarus, unique to the Gospel of John, finds new meaning in queer theology as a powerful archetypal story with the theme of resurrection and coming out.[44] That Jesus calls Lazarus out of the tomb by name is an act of abundant love on the part of Jesus. With John 3:16 and Jesus' commandment to love (13:31–35), we are charged to embody radical love of all persons. Loving God cannot be separated from loving others. Lazarus is called out to a full life, restored and reconciled to relationship, set free from the bindings that held him in death. As Benjamin Perkins remarks, "As I enter the text, I am struck by its unrelenting power to convey that life can come from a lifeless situation and existence, which has deep resonances for anyone who has lived a closeted existence." In Lazarus's unbinding, he is then able to let go of what society has placed on him.[45] The theme of resurrection has been important for gay men with AIDS, who, with drug therapies, once "at death's door have been brought back to life."[46]

The raising of Lazarus also points to the role of the community in coming alongside and supporting those coming out. "I take seriously Jesus' command to 'come out.' I also take equally seriously Jesus' command to those surrounding Lazarus to 'unbind him, and let him go!'" The importance of the response of the community cannot be underestimated. While Lazarus "must answer the call to come out," it is "the community who must unbind him. Such a reimagination reminds us that coming out is far from an individual event; it must take place in community." Again in the words of Perkins, "God has called me out of the lifeless existence of the closet, I have answered this call, and I have continued the journey, thanks to the communities that have unbound me."[47]

Mona West, as a lesbian of faith, resonates deeply with Martha in the story of the raising of Lazarus, understanding Martha's conversation with Jesus and then the grave stone being rolled away as an "invitation to fullness of life." As Martha moves beyond acceptance, queer persons can also move beyond "it's okay to be queer and Christian" to "a radical fullness of grace that empowers me to embody a queer Christ to the world." Martha's own stone is rolled away in another unbinding. West goes on to say,

> John 11 is really Martha's coming out story as a disciple of Jesus. She is invited to trust in her own experience of Jesus. She is also invited to move beyond a mere confession of faith and to accept the radical fullness of Jesus' grace. Her conversation with him thus not only forms the theological heart of the story, it is also at the theological heart of coming out for Christian lesbians and gay men. The first stages of our coming out process often involve tension between faith and complaint. We come to believe through struggle and questioning—involving the same kind of confrontation with Jesus that Martha had in v. 21—that we can be queer and Christian, and that Jesus is the one who is our source of life.[48]

The reaction to the raising of Lazarus is another point of connection from a queer perspective. The raising of Lazarus is the impetus for the decision to kill both Jesus (11:45–53) and Lazarus (12:9–11). The reaction to those who come out is frequently sadly similar. "Coming out is a countercultural and subversive act that threatens the status quo; it can cause religious and governmental leaders to take action against us, even kill us."[49]

A final feature of John's Gospel of which queer interpretation takes notice is the relationship between Jesus and the Beloved Disciple (13:23). Regardless of the identity of the Beloved Disciple, the intimacy between him and Jesus is unmistakable. Gay men historically "have intuited a homoerotic relationship between Jesus and the Beloved Disciple."[50] While the predominance of scholarship on John conflates the Beloved Disciple with a historical person, such as the author of the Gospel, or interprets him as a symbolic figure, a queer reading challenges these heterosexist readings.[51]

Preaching on the relationship between Jesus and the disciple whom he loved is potentially a rare occurrence in the church. The introduction of the Beloved Disciple (13:23) is omitted from the Revised Common Lectionary's Gospel reading for Maundy Thursday (although John 13:21–32 is in the RCL for the Wednesday of Holy Week in all three years), "One of his disciples—the one whom Jesus loved—was reclining next to him" (v. 23). While a portion of chapter 13 (vv. 1–17, 31b–35) is the designated Gospel reading for Maundy Thursday, the story of Jesus washing the disciples' feet takes center stage. It is up to the preacher to determine when a sermon on this character unique to John is demanded, or especially needed by queer folk who connect deeply with the Beloved Disciple. While the relationship between Jesus and the Beloved Disciple "is ambiguous enough for a nonsexual as well as a sexual reading," as the disciple reclines on the breast/bosom/chest of Jesus, "there is a recognized sexual intimacy between Jesus and the beloved disciple at this final meal."[52] This sexual intimacy could easily be missed when the majority of English translations render the Greek word *kolpos* as "heart" or "side" when the word is more accurately translated as breast/bosom/chest. The only other occurrence of *kolpos* in the Gospel of John is to describe the relationship between Jesus and God: "No one has ever seen God. It is God the only Son, who is close to the Father's heart, who has made him known" (1:18).

The Beloved Disciple's love for and loyalty to Jesus is critical to the events of Jesus' passion and resurrection. The Beloved Disciple stands with Jesus' mother at the foot of the cross, and we can imagine "how painful it was for the beloved disciple to watch the man he loved be crucified."[53] The Beloved Disciple along with Peter, at the behest of Mary Magdalene, goes to see Jesus' empty tomb. The Beloved Disciple is again mentioned at the conclusion of the Gospel (21:20–25). "For many queer folks, the Beloved Disciple serves as a reminder how faithful we have been to the Christian tradition despite its exclusions, its violence and its crucifixions of our folks."[54]

HOMILETICAL IMPLICATIONS

As a preacher and an interpreter of the Bible, it is essential to be aware of the terminological distinctions, arguments, and definitions for the queer community, because these are people sitting in your pews. There are pastoral implications when it comes to preaching about LGBTQIA+ lives and bringing a queer perspective to our interpretations of Scripture. Our silence from the pulpit about LGBTQIA+ persons also silences them. They wonder if there is a place for them in the church, if their voices can be heard, especially when the church has historically been hostile toward queer persons and still is. Regardless of denominational arguments made in support of queer people and even denominational decisions to ordain LGBTQIA+ persons, homophobia and transphobia are systemic realities. As the Bible has been used to argue against women's ordination and women's leadership roles in the church, even to validate subordinationism and complementarianism, so also we know how much the Bible gets trotted out to condemn LGBTQIA+ persons without any scriptural, historical, theoretical, or scientific awareness or knowledge.

The church leader, the preacher, is responsible for being aware of the passages used against LGBTQIA+ persons and being able to speak to them. Like those stories in the Bible that have frightened women, those passages that have been weaponized to validate the view of women as property, to rationalize rape, to subordinate women, to accept sexism and misogyny, queer persons also have their "texts of terror."[55] This is true, of course, for any group historically marginalized by Scripture. It is the preacher's ethical responsibility to speak into those passages that oppress, including, but not limited to, texts that support the subjugation of women, the justification of slavery, the condoning of racism and white privilege, the perpetuation of xenophobia, and the rationalization of anti-Semitism.

When bringing a queer perspective into the pulpit, the preacher must also be aware of the kind of tone communicated about queer lives, queer theology, and queer perspectives. As Linn Marie Tonstad notes, too often the stance is apologetic,[56] that is, a tone of defensiveness rather than an active projection of support or, as this chapter suggests, demonstrative engagement with Scripture in the pulpit from a queer perspective. It is one thing to make a case to justify queer perspectives and biblical interpretation for the sake of preaching. It is another thing altogether to engage actively in such an approach so that people can hear the difference it makes for the meaning of Scripture. A preacher might ask how allyship for our queer siblings can be demonstrated in our preaching.

Being gendered and sexual beings is part and parcel of what it means to be human. The humanity of Jesus is the unique claim of Christianity as how God chose to reveal God's self—in human flesh. And yet, the church—and its preaching—has a long history of compartmentalizing the humanity of the faithful and the humanity of Jesus. A homiletical implication of a queer interpretation of Scripture mandates that preachers reflect on our avoidance of sex, gender, and sexual ethics in the pulpit. Likely many of us do not want to think or preach about such things when it comes to Jesus, lest we offend those who try to cordon off their sexuality from a life of faith.

Sexual ethics are a part of the Christian faith and of Christian living.

When we do not speak about sex, gender, and our bodies from the pulpit we implicitly communicate that sex is taboo; that the topic has nothing to do with how we live our lives before God; that God is not a part of that aspect of being human; that it does not belong in conversations about faith. Gender and sexuality are fundamental to what it means to be human. If the preacher decides to be silent, that does not mean that the conversation has gone quiet. Our people will find other voices and other places where honest dialogue and intimate sharing can be had.

The church's history of monitoring sexuality is also at play. "The current crisis of the Church surrounding sexuality will continue because our conversations are often not guided by faith but by the will to control."[57] When the church is silent when it comes to sex and sexual ethics, it then is silent about basic human relationship. Take, for example, how we talk about divorce—we don't, afraid of upsetting people, and rightly so. A text like Mark 10:2–12 should not be read out loud in a worship setting without a sermon that tackles the passage head-on.

To an extent we have so divinized Jesus that any discussion about sex and sexuality has no place in Christian dialogue. And yet, Jesus was the Word made flesh. As Tonstad notes, "Theology talks about a God the Father and a God the Son, but pretends fatherhood and sonship have nothing to do with sex or gender even as Christianity has also (but not only) been a system of patriarchy throughout its history."[58]

An important critique of our preaching from the perspective of queer hermeneutics is the homiletical practice of inclusive language or inclusivity in talking about or referring to God. Preachers try to be sensitive to issues of sexuality and gender when it comes to interpreting and preaching the Bible by showing the feminine side, feminine attributes, or feminine images of God. And yet, these attributes are themselves socially constructed. As a result, the preacher "repeats, rather than destabilizes, the core heterosexual masculinity that God is often given."[59]

A queer interpretive approach assists preachers in recognizing their own heteronormativity that is present in their language, their interpretation of Scripture, the workings of their congregations and communities of faith, even the examples or stories used in sermons. Heteronormativity as "the institutionalized preference for opposite-sex sexual relationships over same-sex sexual relationships" is as systemic as racism and sexism. It assumes additional beliefs and practices that deeply affect social constructions having to do with acceptable sexual desire, activity, and practices.[60] These are the presuppositions in play for our people and how they relate to each other, and even to God.

When it comes to preaching the Gospel of John, knowing that there are members of your congregation who identify as LGBTQIA+, how will this Gospel be heard? Is this a homiletical opportunity to lift up this perspective of John, not only for the pastoral care of your LGBTQIA+ people, but also to challenge heteronormativity? If Christianity is concerned with identity, a concern inherent both to Christianity's self-reflective capacity and to its growth, then sexuality and gender cannot be sidelined. Gender and sexuality are central to humanity. "To become a human being means to become a sexed and gendered person, with a sexuality that is central to our authentic humanity and that, if 'repressed' . . . , will express itself in one way or another, possibly damaging us in the process."[61] As the church already has a history of damaging its believers with doctrine antithetical to its central tenets, preaching would do well to recommit itself to not perpetuating such damage.

FURTHER RESOURCES FOR PREACHING

Askew, Emily, and O. Wesley Allen Jr. *Beyond Heterosexism in the Pulpit*. Eugene, OR: Cascade Books, 2015.
Hinnant, Olive Elaine. *God Comes Out: A Queer Homiletic*. Cleveland: Pilgrim Press, 2007.

7

Ecological Interpretation

INTRODUCTION

An opening question in the preface to *The Green Bible* centralizes the primary concern of an ecological approach to the interpretation of the Bible: "What is my role as a Christian in caring for the earth?"[1] Creation, the created order, and God as Creator have always been a part of Christian theological imagination. The creation stories in Genesis show the interconnectedness between creation and humanity. After all, "God so loved the world (cosmos)." The Bible abounds with ecological references, and the ecological settings for the stories of Scripture shape meaning. "Creation theology teaches that throughout the Bible the allusions to land, water, and air; fish, birds, and beasts; barrenness and fertility; and famine, rain, and food are not meaningless or empty."[2]

An ecological hermeneutic observes the evolution of how ecology is defined. While ecology was once largely perused from a purely scientific view, ecology is now integrated with the entirety of human existence and function. Climate change and the climate crisis have made the ecological interpretive question all the more acute. An ecological hermeneutic for the interpretation of the Bible comes to the forefront because of these converging climate crises. Beyond the political debates and divisions, what will be the Christian response to the groaning of creation? Direct attention to how the Bible is relevant in such discourse is but one result of the environmental crises engulfing planet Earth. An ecological hermeneutic is "taking a stand at the side of suffering creation."[3] Norman Habel names an additional "contributing factor" to a focus on ecological criticism as a general "Earth consciousness." After astronauts photographed Earth from space, Earth became more than just a sphere of resources for the taking.

If ecological interpretation is an environmental response, how will we then define "environment" from a Christian perspective? Francis Watson argues that a Christian perspective understands environment as creation, "that is, as originating in the creative act of the triune God who is the subject and object of the fundamental biblical and credal narrative." At the same time, the environmental concern and response are shaping Christian theology. "A Christian understanding of 'creation' will now be affected by the current concept of 'environment,' with its connotations of fragility, finitude, interdependence and inherent worth."[4]

One of the challenges of an ecological hermeneutic, therefore, is that it calls for reevaluation of central Christian theological tenets. We have to be willing to question and even reformulate basic Christian doctrines to make a biblical case for care of the environment. Even the role of Jesus gets recast from an ecological perspective. Jesus' ministry is also about a concern for "the creatureliness" that humanity shares "with the rest of the natural or created order."[5] At stake for ecological interpretation is the belief that God's created order is threatened by our inattention to the environment, creation, and the ecological harmony of the universe. "Therefore the environmental crisis must be seen as a profound religious crisis; it is a massive disordering of our relationship with the God who created heaven and earth."[6]

SUMMARY OF THE APPROACH

Whereas the historical-critical model of biblical interpretation has viewed the Bible as an object of study, ecological interpretation is "not an exploration of what a given text may say *about* creation, *about* nature, or *about* Earth."[7] That is, the earth is not a theme for analysis. The earth is "a voice or (often marginalized) presence in the text that has to be listened to. In this way, earth becomes a subject (with a voice in its own right) and not so much a theme (topos) in the biblical texts."[8] Earth is our home, our habitat, and we read Scripture with a commitment to our solidarity with the earth. Ecological interpretation imagines a kind of partnership or kinship with the earth, a stance of accompaniment, advocacy, and allyship. It is a "reflecting *with* the earth and not so much *about* the earth, in the same way that feminist biblical scholars would want to read the Bible in solidarity *with* oppressed women and not *for* them."[9] As such, the interpretive method for ecological approaches has been twofold: to respond to the critique that Christianity itself is at fault for the ecological crisis because of its anthropocentrism and to argue that the Bible offers "ecological wisdom but that this has all too often remained hidden or implicit."[10]

Norman Habel maintains that what is essential, therefore, is a "critical hermeneutic of suspicion, identification, and retrieval." By having a hermeneutic of suspicion, we admit that the biblical writers and therefore the biblical texts are "inherently anthropocentric" and have "traditionally been read from an anthropocentric perspective" or with an "anthropocentric bias."[11] Habel names two aspects of this anthropocentric bias. The first is that "in the hierarchy of things there is a God, human beings, and the rest of creation." There is a pecking order, and we as human beings believe that we come in first. And second, we tend to view nature as an object of "human investigation," all the while underscoring "a sense of superiority over nature" and "a sense of distance, separation, and otherness."[12] Ecological interpretation exposes "the biases in readers and the texts that have generated an understanding of nonhuman entities as objects, thus creating a sense of distance from these nonhuman entities which are seen as other and alien."[13] Recognizing the inherent anthropomorphic bias in the biblical writers and in the Bible's interpreters, we begin to see a pattern of focusing "on human events, contexts, and relationships rather than the natural habitat, environment, or entities imbedded in the text."[14]

The next critical hermeneutical move is identification. Habel defines identification as having empathy with earth. While we tend to identify with human characters, with this approach, we identify with nonhuman figures, specifically identifying with the earth "as a presence, character, or voice in the text." The third critical interpretive stance is retrieval, which is an "attempt to recover the voice of the Earth (capitalized as a character) even where this is silenced or opposed by the explicit perspective of the text."[15] The Earth Bible Project names six aims guiding ecological hermeneutics driven by ecojustice principles. These aims and principles provide a helpful taxonomy for preachers who want to engage an ecological hermeneutic. The Earth Bible Project aims to acknowledge that:

1. ". . . as Western interpreters we are heirs of a long anthropocentric, patriarchal, and androcentric approach . . . that has devalued the Earth" with the underlying principle being the "intrinsic worth" of the universe, Earth, and all its components.
2. as humans, we have "exploited, oppressed, and endangered the existence of the Earth community."
3. we need to be aware of the fact that "we are also members of the endangered Earth community in dialogue with ancient texts." We exist in interconnectedness with Earth and all its living things.
4. the earth is "a subject in the text with which we seek to relate empathetically rather than as a topic to be analyzed rationally."
5. it is our call "to take up the cause of justice for Earth," to partner with Earth toward balance and purposes as part of a "dynamic cosmic design."
6. that we seek "to discern and retrieve alternative traditions where the voice of Earth has been suppressed."[16] Earth indeed has a voice that speaks out against the injustices it has endured.

Ecological hermeneutics restores the earth to its created and creating status as that which God loves, not as an object of study, like ecology and theology, but as a crying voice that gives witness to God's work in the world.

SAMPLE TEXT: JOHN 18:1–12

The sample text to illustrate interpretive possibilities from an ecological viewpoint is the arrest of Jesus in the Gospel of John.[17] John's version includes a detail about the setting absent from the Synoptic Gospels—that the arrest of Jesus takes place outside a *garden*. The "garden of Gethsemane" is known well by the Christian masses and preachers alike as the location where Jesus, after sharing a meal with his disciples on the night of his betrayal, prayed, "Let this cup pass/Remove this cup" (Matt. 26:39; Mark 14:36, respectively). It is a rare Christian indeed who is not familiar with the portrait of Jesus' "agony in the garden." Having gone off alone to pray, leaving his disciples behind, Jesus is pictured with his hands clasped, leaning on a rock, gazing upward. Hanging in churches, pastors' studies, a grandmother's living room, Heinrich Hofmann's *Christ in Gethsemane* (1886) has taken on an interpretive life of its own. Yet, both "garden of Gethsemane" and "agony in the garden" necessitate a harmonization of John with Matthew and Mark. Luke's account of Jesus' arrest has Jesus and his disciples going to the Mount of Olives but does not mention Gethsemane, as do Matthew and Mark. In the Synoptic Gospels, Jesus' agony is exacerbated by the disciples' inability to remain awake while he prays. In Luke, Jesus departs from his disciples once to pray alone. In Matthew and Mark, Jesus leaves his disciples to pray by himself and then returns not once but three times, each time finding them asleep (Matt. 26:40–46; Mark 14:37–41; Luke 22:45–46). Jesus' agony is further intensified by the knowledge Jesus brings with him to his prayers— during the Passover meal with his disciples, Jesus has already predicted both Judas's betrayal and Peter's denial.

The Fourth Evangelist alters the chronology of the events prior to Jesus' arrest. While the Synoptic Gospels have Jesus praying once he and the disciples arrive at the location of Jesus' arrest, in John, Jesus prays with his disciples present while they are still in the space where they shared a meal. Only after the prayer do Jesus and his disciples cross the Kidron Valley (18:1), which separates the eastern wall of Jerusalem's Old City/Temple Mount and the Mount of Olives. John does not mention the Mount of Olives but narrates that Jesus "went out with his disciples across the Kidron valley to a place where there was a garden, which he and his disciples entered" (v. 1). Once in the garden, Jesus neither prays nor asks for the cup to pass. Instead, in response to Peter's cutting off the right ear of the high priest's slave, Malchus, Jesus says, "Am I not to drink the cup that the Father has given me?" (v. 11). There is no "agony in the garden" according to John because Jesus has already experienced five chapters of agony in the Farewell Discourse (chaps. 13–17). Once Jesus arrives at the garden, the agony is not necessarily over, but the focus for the Fourth Gospel is how Jesus will now fulfill his identity as the gate and the Good Shepherd from chapter 10.

In John, Judas's betrayal has already happened when he exited the room, abandoning both his friends and Jesus (13:30). Only six verses later, Jesus predicts Peter's denial (vv. 36–38). The Farewell Discourse is a compendium of emotions as Jesus prepares his disciples for what is to come, and Jesus' heart is just as troubled as those of his disciples (14:1). The garden, on the other hand, is where the divinity of Jesus takes the front stage. Jesus does not wait for Judas to identify him to the authorities, and there is no kiss of betrayal in John. Jesus willingly comes out of the garden. While most translations say that Jesus "came forward," a more accurate rendering of the Greek verb is "came out," thereby leaving the disciples, the sheep, safely in the garden, the fold. As the Good Shepherd (10:11–18), Jesus willingly hands himself over to the Roman soldiers and the police representing the chief priest and the Pharisees. As the gate/door, Jesus puts himself between the disciples and the soldiers who have come "with lanterns and torches and weapons" (18:3). Jesus places himself at the opening to the garden, protecting his sheep from the intruders—the thieves, bandits, strangers, and wolves—who only come "to steal and kill and destroy" (10:10).

The garden is a familiar place—"Jesus often met there with his disciples" (18:2)—and it is a safe space. An ecological perspective might "make explicit the Palestinian ecological context that the Gospels largely take for granted in the hope of discovering something of Jesus' relationship with it."[18] What is Jesus' connection with this garden? Why bring his disciples to this place, at this time? What is Jesus trying to show his disciples at this moment of his kingdom not of this world (v. 36)? What might Jesus be communicating to his disciples about the events that are to follow, which his arrest will set in motion? Does the meaning of the passion narrative then include "the whole of creation" and perhaps signify the "redemption of the human relationship with the rest of creation"?[19]

From an ecological viewpoint, place and habitat matter. Only after God makes habitable the inhabitable can creatures come into view.[20] The garden setting of Jesus' arrest has a unique purpose in John's Gospel as the place where Jesus confirms his identity and reveals who he truly is to the world. "Whom are you looking for?" says Jesus (John v. 4). When the mob answers, "Jesus of Nazareth" (v. 5), Jesus then utters the last two absolute "I am" statements in the Gospel (vv. 6, 8).[21] While English translations include "he" after "I am," the pronoun does not exist in the Greek text. The truth of Jesus' identity is made clear— Jesus is God, the I AM, in the flesh, echoing Exodus. "But Moses said to God, 'If I come to the Israelites and say to them, "The God of your ancestors has sent me to you," and they ask me, "What is his name?" what shall I say to them?' God said to Moses, 'I AM WHO I AM.' He said further, 'Thus you shall say to the Israelites, "I AM has sent me to you"'" (Exod. 3:13–14). God is in the garden, reconciling the whole world (the Roman soldiers, the Jewish police), the entire cosmos (John 3:16), to relationship with God.

That Jesus' arrest takes place in a garden also foreshadows his death, burial, and resurrection. Only in John do Jesus' crucifixion, burial, and resurrection take place near or in a garden: "Now there was a garden in the place where he was crucified, and in the garden there was a new tomb in which no one had ever been laid" (19:41). The appearance of the resurrected Jesus to Mary Magdalene, therefore, happens in a garden. Through an ecological perspective, the garden represents new life, resurrected life. The garden is a place of relationship between the divine and the human—between Jesus and his disciples at his arrest and between Jesus and Mary Magdalene at his resurrection. "Jesus is the gardener, arisen to redeem all of creation. Christ the gardener has returned."[22]

The mention of a garden is also an allusion to soil and its life-giving properties—even the soil from which the first human was formed.

> Being fully human means also understanding our unbreakable bond with the land, the material base of life. One cannot go more than a few chapters in the Old Testament without seeing some vivid reference to land and its importance for humanity, beginning with the image of *adam* (Heb., "man, humankind") formed from *adamah* ("soil") in Genesis 2:7. That wordplay suggests a kind of familial connection; it is a subtle yet powerful reminder that the life of people comes from its land.[23]

The life-giving properties of soil and dirt are demonstrated in Jesus' healing of the man born blind. "When [Jesus] had said this, he spat on the ground and made mud with the saliva and spread the mud on the man's eyes, saying to him, 'Go, wash in the pool of Siloam' (which means Sent). Then he went and washed and came back able to see" (John 9:6–7).

From an ecological perspective, the mutual interpretive possibilities between the garden, soil, the healing of the man born blind, and the allusion to Genesis 2:7 then also bring to light the role of the Holy Spirit in John in the theme of creation. When Jesus appears to his disciples who have hidden themselves behind locked doors in the wake of his arrest, trial, crucifixion, and burial, Jesus gives them the Holy Spirit. While most translations read, "he breathed on them" (20:22), a more accurate rendition is, "he breathed *into* them." The verb, *emphysaō*, is the same verb used in the Septuagint in Genesis 2:7, "Then the LORD God formed man from the dust of the ground, and breathed into his nostrils the breath of life; and the man became a living being," and in Ezekiel 37:9, "Then he said to me, 'Prophesy to the breath, prophesy, mortal, and say to the breath: Thus says the Lord GOD: Come from the four winds, O breath, and breathe upon these slain, that they may live.'" What is happening in the garden will have an impact on all of creation.

Furthermore, the garden in Jesus' arrest scene is an allusion to the opening verses of John's Gospel. The first words of John, "in the beginning," are the same as the first words of the book of Genesis in the Septuagint, the Greek translation of the Old Testament. The Septuagint would have been John's Scripture, as the Gospel writers composed in Greek in a completely hellenized first-century Palestine. By quoting the opening phrase of Genesis, the Fourth Evangelist situates Jesus' "birth," death, and resurrection within creation and the created order. The Word made flesh as from God and with God (John 1:1) is also "in the beginning with God. All things came into being through him, and without him not one thing came into being" (vv. 2–3). In the garden, things are coming into being once again. The Word made flesh brings about new creation, a restoration of creation. With the allusion to Genesis, echoes of the garden of Eden are unmistakable.

We human creatures are intimately connected to creation and our Creator. That Jesus will take away the sin of the world (v. 29) means a restoration of the broken relationship between humans and God from the beginning of time.[24] The purpose of the Word becoming flesh, of Jesus' life and ministry, of Jesus' death, resurrection, and ascension, is relationship with God as children of God (vv. 12–13).

When these allusions to the first two chapters of Genesis are noted, the most famous verse of John's Gospel comes into different focus. While the tendency is to interpret "for God so loved the world" with "world" representing humanity, the Greek word is *kosmos*. The semantic domain of garden, breath/spirit, creation, *kosmos* suggests that Jesus is restoring not just humanity's relationship with God, but humanity's relationship with the cosmos, the created order. Through the lens of an ecological perspective, the garden becomes a character that beckons humanity back to relationship with its creator.

HOMILETICAL IMPLICATIONS

A quote attributed to Irenaeus, "The initial step for a soul to come to knowledge of God is contemplation of nature," would resonate with many, if not most, Christians. "Finding God in nature" is an oft-uttered description of a believer's relationship with God. Ecological criticism can help preachers expand on this assumption and hope. While it is true that the biblical writers were not attentive to our ecological awarenesses, an ecological interpretive approach yields a number of homiletical implications for preaching, as "more than ever, readers are looking to texts to explain not only the changes in the environment but also what the appropriate response is to these changes." An ecological perspective "offers a way of reading the biblical texts that elevates earth and its nonhuman communities to active participants in the ongoing business of life; at the same time, it raises awareness of the intricate relationship between earth and humans."[25]

First, an ecological perspective becomes an important corrective of the ways in which Christian theology has centered on the individual. "Jesus is my personal Lord and Savior" is the mantra for many a Christian. The anthropocentrism of dominant trends in Christian theology has dangerously morphed into autonomy and even selfishness. In Genesis, "the great blessing, 'Be fruitful and multiply,' is spoken to fish and birds on the fifth day (1:22),"[26] before it is spoken to Adam and Eve. Indeed, a careful reading of the creation story in Genesis confirms that humans are not the center of the universe. Day six of creation is not all about us. "And God said, 'Let the earth bring forth living creatures of every kind: cattle and creeping things and wild animals of the earth of every kind.' And it was so. God made the wild animals of the earth of every kind, and the cattle of every kind, and everything that creeps upon the ground of every kind. And God saw that it was good" (1:24–26). Only after the cows are humans then made.

Ecology is not just a scientific category but theological expression. God reveals who God is through the ecological systems of our world. God's choice of revelation is through the created order. Ecological interpretation pays attention to how images from creation and the environment themselves communicate theology and notes how central this is to the way the biblical writers seek to capture God at work. The images are not a means to an end but critical for communicating theological truths about God as creator. The biblical writers communicate that to know nature, to know creation, is to know God.

Ecological interpretation of the Bible is an important critique of eschatological tenets in Christianity, especially when focused more on "saving souls for heaven, rather than on saving Earth for living."[27] Ironically, central beliefs in Christianity have worked against theological ecology. These "stumbling blocks in the way of creation-keeping discipleship,"[28] for example, an eschatology that favors heaven and everlasting life, keep an ecological hermeneutic at bay. Ecological inter-pretation calls into question the reinterpretation of central Christian doctrinal foci. When the primary area of focus is eschatological con-cerns, does the earth really need protecting or care? If the end times are coming soon, "preserving the earth is hardly a priority and may even represent opposition to the progress of God's eschatological pur-poses."[29] A reaccounting of ecology as a theological category is gospel proclamation. "This is the good news. God's plan for the redemption of the earth is no less bold or powerful than his [*sic*] original, creative one. The difference is that, although we were not part of his original creative team, we are invited to be on the redemptive one. Caring for creation is not a new theology; rather, it has simply been forgotten."[30]

Ecological hermeneutics also calls for a reevaluation of the Chris-tian doctrine of the fall. Concerns about the environment in inter-pretation of the Bible have revealed "a seriously deficient construal of Christian faith and the biblical witness" in the fall/redemption model. While "creation is affirmed," it is not "an integral part of the main story. Creation is merely the stage on which the real drama of fall and redemption is played out." More important than humans being created is the fact that though fallen, they are redeemed. This model becomes the working hermeneutic for the entirety of Scripture, and the rela-tionship between the divine and humans takes center stage. This is not just an anthropocentric view, because "anthropocentrism is inescapable for humans." Rather, it is anthropomonistic. "It is as though the Bible started at Genesis 3."[31]

A historical focus on the fall and subsequent redemption in Chris-tian theology means undue emphasis on human sin in Christian the-ology. Ecological interpretation asks how the concentration on human sin has dwarfed other components of biblical theology that could be viewed as "glorious new unfoldings of continuing creation," such as election, redemption, revelation, salvation, and eschaton.[32] "For much of Western Christianity, the doctrine of creation (a biblical term) has been eaten alive by the doctrine of the fall (not a biblical term). In other words, creation's downfall resulting from human sin has eclipsed its original glow as God's handiwork, radiant with God's glory." In this "exaggerated doctrine of the fall, God's creation loses its sacredness as God's beloved artwork" and "we have magnified human sin beyond sane bounds."[33]

An ecological approach provides preachers with opportunities to talk about stewardship, discipleship, and vocation. In our attempts to redeem Genesis 1:26–28 and taking care of the garden in 2:15, the Christian doctrine of stewardship is used to interpret human dominion. But "nowhere does the Bible say that humans are appointed stewards of creation."[34] Ecological approaches ask to what extent Genesis 1:28, "God blessed them, and God said to them, 'Be fruitful and multiply, and fill the earth and subdue it; and have dominion over the fish of the sea and over the birds of the air and over every living thing that moves upon the earth,'" has become a license for a no-holds-barred perspective of the role of humanity in the created order. This is not only anthropocentrism gone awry, but a problematic reading of the meaning of dominion. "Dominion as outright oppression is not advocated or condoned in Scripture," but rather dominion is "responsible stewardship."[35] An ecological perspective can prevent stewardship from being repackaged colonialism.

Jesus' last "I am" statement with a predicate nominative, "I am the vine, you are the branches" (John 15:5), highlights the interconnectedness of Jesus' own sense of stewardship, which is not about rule or dominion. How preachers speak about and define stewardship as care for the earth all too often leads to distancing ourselves from that interconnectedness. We might reposition stewardship as responsive "activism"—embodying a theology of creation in our lives.

In the aftermath of a global pandemic, an ecological approach to biblical interpretation confirms what the pandemic exposed—the far-reaching interconnectedness of our world. Countries like to maintain a certain level of sovereignty and yet quickly realized how impossible that aspiration truly is. At the same time, we also exist in an interconnected universe. "There is no such thing as running 'away' or throwing anything 'away' in an interconnected universe. What goes around, whether it is a physical pollutant or a spiritual one, ultimately comes around. This is the character of the creator God's world."[36] The pandemic also exposed the vulnerability of the poor in our society. Having an ecological sensitivity when reading the Bible is another avenue for talking about care for the poor, when the poor and oppressed are adversely affected by climate change. "The poor and the vulnerable are members of God's family and are the most severely affected by droughts, high temperatures, the flooding of coastal cities, and more severe and unpredictable weather events resulting from climate change."[37] In these current realities, attention to ecological themes in Scripture could gain more traction as the pandemic revealed our total inability to sector off our lives from creation. Ecology is theology, for "to be human is to be a creature and a member of the community of creation. It is also to be made in the image of God, that is, to participate in the fulfilment of human creatureliness in Jesus, the incarnate Word."[38]

FURTHER RESOURCES FOR PREACHING

Habel, Norman C., David Rhoads, and H. Paul Santmire, eds. *The Season of Creation: A Preaching Commentary*. Minneapolis: Fortress Press, 2011.

Holbert, John C. *Preaching Creation: The Environment and the Pulpit*. Eugene, OR: Cascade Books, 2011.

Schade, Leah D. Creation-Crisis *Preaching: Ecology, Theology, and the Pulpit*. St. Louis: Chalice Press, 2015.

8

The Bible and Disability

INTRODUCTION

Disability studies, like feminist and race studies, "stands at the intersection of political activism and academia."[1] It arose in the 1960s and 1970s as persons with disabilities began actively to protest systemic discrimination and generalized categorization.

The medical framework that historically dominated disability perspectives presumed a need for treatment or correction arising from medical diagnoses, focusing on "cure, rehabilitation, and adjustment"; the discourse was "*for/on* rather than *with/by* people with disabilities."[2] The medical model ends up placing the challenge of disability on the person with the disability.[3] Early scholarship of the Bible engaged the medical model of disability, and yet this framework was largely unknown to the biblical world.[4]

The limits of a medical model for disability studies moved the conversation to a social model, recognizing "how social, political, religious, environmental, and other structures contribute to the experience of disability."[5] This model examines the "social oppression, cultural discourse, and environmental barriers rather than biological deficit and claims that it is the constrictions and inadequacies of society that disable the individual."[6] In other words, disability "refers to the social and structural discrimination that people with impairments face."[7] In this model, the problem is located in these social and political realities that block full citizenship of impaired persons.[8] Out of this model comes the important terminological distinction between "impairment (a physiological, medical phenomenon) and disability (a social phenomenon)."[9] *Impairment* "refers to a biological anomaly that inhibits the body from functioning normatively."[10]

The social model for disability studies was critiqued "for defining disability as socially constructed discrimination comparable to racism, sexism, or homophobia." The essential criticism of the social model was that "disability is not just a matter of discrimination since the bodies and minds of people with impairments do not function like the minds and bodies of the nondisabled."[11]

The cultural model critiques the inherent binaries of the social model, arguing that disability is determined by "cultural rules" based on normed expectations of bodies. Disability is thus seen as "a product of the ways that cultures use physical and cognitive differences to narrate, organize, and interpret their world." Put another way, "descriptions of disability become one way by which we create or shape culture."[12] With this cultural lens comes "insights about cultural categories, ideas of otherness, and social groups' access to or lack of power."[13] The cultural model recognizes that "disability is made up of a complex variety of cultural factors, which might include medical issues and social discrimination, but it is not limited to these factors." Rather than provide a succinct definition of disability, the cultural model analyzes how a particular culture navigates disability and able-bodied.[14]

Out of this model arises the term "normate" in disability studies, "to describe the veiled subject position from which the disabled as a figure of otherness is constructed."[15] Disability studies, like gender studies, also calls forth an "intersectional" perspective. "The central notion of intersectionality is that mutually reinforcing vectors of power and oppression, such as race, gender, class, and sexuality, must be taken into account in order to understand the complexity of hierarchical relations."[16] All persons find themselves in more than one category, both contemporarily and in the ancient world. A disability approach pays attention to how identifiers, particularly around power (such as race, gender, class, economy, and age), intersect with disability. It is the cultural model that has been the most prominent in biblical studies.

An important consideration for disability approaches is language. Contemporary sensitivies concerning persons with disabilities have introduced terms such as "physically challenged." Amos Yong suggests that this new terminology betrays our own discomfort with the differently abled. Yong also proposes that we say "persons with disabilities" rather than "the disabled" because we are "people first, and with or without disabilities second."[17] Our language to designate persons with disabilities also exposes our normative biases, assuming that ability is the norm. Just as racism privileges whiteness and sexism privileges maleness, ableism privileges nondisabled existence, exposing an embedded worldview against persons who are disabled. Defining "ableism" is critical, therefore, in understanding the dominant culture's bigotry against differently abled persons. Ableism "names the discriminatory attitudes, negative stereotypes, and sociopolitical and economic structures and institutions that together function to exclude people with disabilities from full participation in society."[18]

The term "disability" itself is ambiguous. With many types of disability, a more general understanding of disability best captures the spectrum. Intellectual and physical disabilities can be attributed to multiple issues, resulting from chronic illnesses or diseases or sudden tragedies or onsets. This generalization enables persons to locate themselves from their particular circumstances. In the end, "the term *disability* is a modern category" and having an "open-ended"[19] understanding of the term becomes essential, especially in biblical interpretation, so as not to place modern constructs onto ancient texts. "Disability," therefore, can be used for people who "potentially may have faced restrictions on their ability to carry out everyday activities through injury, disease, congenital malformation, aging or chronic illness, or whose appearance made them liable to be characterized by contemporary cultural ideals associated with non-standard bodies."[20] Establishing "a" disability hermeneutic, therefore, is a "bit unwieldy."[21]

SUMMARY OF THE APPROACH

Only in the last two decades have disability approaches been a voice in biblical interpretation. Navigating the complexity of how the Bible negotiates disability means that there is no one methodology at play. Depending on the interpretive goal, the approach might seek to pay "attention to terminology and literary representation, to critique of normate tendencies in previous scholarship," or to offer "constructive rereadings in an effort to 'reclaim the identity of those stigmatized as "other."'"[22]

As the term "disability" itself is a modern category, no term exists for "disabled" in Greek, Hebrew, or Latin, and there is "limited data on persons with disabilities in the ancient Near East."[23] The wide array of disability in the Bible includes an assortment of impairments (e.g., blindness, muteness), demon possession, and even infertility or barrenness; disabilities from birth, from injury (including abuse and violence), from illness, from age, from mental illness, as well as intellectual and developmental disabilities.[24] From this multifaceted vantage point, biblical passages otherwise thought not to raise issues about disability can be interpreted through a disability lens.

Another category under which assessment of disability resides, especially for the interpretation of Christian texts, is the concept of kyriarchy. "To determine what it meant to be disabled in antiquity, it is necessary to ask what other identity categories and power hierarchies intersected with disability in order to affect a person's social location."[25] The *kyrios*—the male householder in the Greco-Roman household codes—was the ideal by which ability and disability were evaluated. Coined by Elisabeth Schüssler Fiorenza, the term *kyriarchy* "underscores that domination is not simply a matter of patriarchal, gender-based dualism but of more comprehensive, interlocking hierarchically ordered structures of domination."[26] The ideal of the *kyrios* is clearly male, but also a most perfect specimen.

In her work on disability in ancient Christian texts, Anna Rebecca Solevåg argues that physiognomy also has been used to interpret the presentation of the body; "outward appearance signified inner moral features." This overlap of disability studies and physiognomy reveals how "people with disabilities have been particularly vulnerable to physiognomic interpretations." From a review of primary texts, Solevåg concludes, "The taxonomy is clear: good-looking men are good, but those with nonnormative bodies betray a deviant soul."[27] This observation becomes especially important when negotiating theological evaluations of disabled biblical characters.

Biblical interpretation from the perspective of disability and disability studies provides a corrective to the ways in which theological claims, particularly about sin, have been negatively connected to persons with disabilities. For biblical interpretation, the task of disability studies is not to question the worldview of the Bible when it comes to persons with disabilities, but our own prejudices toward disabled persons that we bring to our reading of biblical texts.[28] How can the Bible be good news for persons with disabilities? A "disability hermeneutic" is "an approach to the Bible that is informed by the experiences of disability."[29]

It is also important to note the difference between a cure and a healing. In her essay on disability in Johannine literature, Jaime Clark-Soles writes that a cure is "the elimination of impairment and is experienced at the individual level." Healing "refers to a person who has experienced integration and reconciliation to self, God, and the community."[30] Healing, therefore, does not necessarily mean a cure.

Amos Yong identifies three ideas that should advise a hermeneutic of disability. These three issues simultaneously expose the assumptions we hold about persons with disabilities. First, "people with disabilities are created in the image of God that is measured according to the person of Christ." We judge a person's worth based on physical ideals determined by societal standards, and yet our theological beliefs demand otherwise. Second, persons with disabilities are not to be pitied. They do not ask for, nor do they need to be, summed up by their disability alone. They are more than their disability, "agents in their own right." Third, "disabilities are not necessarily evils or blemishes to be eliminated."[31] Persons with disabilities do not need to be fixed and do not always ask or need to be cured.

An approach to the Bible with a hermeneutic of disability in mind ferrets out those interpretations that further marginalize persons with disabilities. It calls attention to where and how readings of texts have excluded or oppressed the differently abled and calls forth correctives that might result in redemption. We cannot reconstruct "what life with a disability was like for most ancient Israelites,"[32] but we can examine how biblical texts and their interpretations culturally express disability. A disability hermeneutic can name the ways in which texts and their interpretations can further marginalize or where texts can potentially liberate.

SAMPLE TEXT: JOHN 9:1–41

In John 9, the healing of a man born blind, we encounter one of the longest stories in Scripture that focuses on a person with a disability.[33] It is one of only three healing stories in the Gospel of John (4:46–54; 5:1–47; 9:1–10:21).[34] The healing of the royal official's son in John 4 and the healing of the man unable to walk for thirty-eight years in John 5 introduce the general term used for illness, disability, or invalid persons—*astheneia*. In John 5, the Fourth Evangelist lists three sub-categories of this term: *typhlos* (blind), *chōlos* (lame), and *xēros* (para-lyzed).[35] The other occurrences of *typhlos* and its lexemes are in chapter 9; chapter 10, "Others were saying, 'These are not the words of one who has a demon.' Can a demon open the eyes of the blind?'" (10:21); in chapter 11, the raising of Lazarus, referring back to the healing of the man born blind (v. 37); and chapter 12, "He has blinded their eyes and hardened their heart, so that they might not look with their eyes, and understand with their heart and turn—and I would heal them" (v. 20).

The story of the man born blind makes up one of the longest textual units in the Gospel of John (9:1–10:21) and follows the structural pattern established by the Fourth Evangelist of sign, dialogue, discourse (already in chaps. 5 and 6). Jesus performs a miracle; following the miracle is dialogue or conversation among the characters involved as they attempt to understand or make sense of what the miracle might mean; the overall event ends with Jesus offering his interpretation of the story, the discourse. For the Fourth Gospel, these miraculous events are not named miracles but "signs." The healings direct our attention to a more important truth about Jesus and for the person being healed. This is often a challenge for making sense of the healing stories in the Gospels. "The nature of most healing stories is such that we either know a lot about Jesus, but very little about the character with the disability, or we know this character only as a paradigm of faithful discipleship."[36]

Before the actual healing itself, there are several issues to address through a disability lens. The opening question from the disciples, "Who sinned?" (9:2), assumes the ancient worldview that physical ailments or disabilities were the result of someone's sin or ancestral sin. Later in the story, the Pharisees repeat this long-held belief. "They answered [the healed man], 'You were born entirely in sins, and are you trying to teach us?' And they drove him out" (v. 34). A disability perspective calls out the abled persons who presume their superiority. The Pharisees think they know more or know better than the formerly blind man.

Jesus' response to the disciples' question is "one that is essential for any contemporary project in rethinking disability at a theological level."[37] The importance of Jesus' answer as undermining the connection between sin and ailments is often mitigated by translational issues that plague the second half of Jesus' response, "he was born blind so that God's works might be revealed in him." The majority of English translations render the *hina* clause as a purpose clause, "so that" or "but it was in order that." That is, the man was born blind *for the purpose of* God's works being revealed in him. Eugene Peterson's *The Message* gets closer to the function of the Greek clause. "Jesus said, "You're asking the wrong question. You're looking for someone to blame. There is no such cause-effect here. Look instead for what God can do." That is, "Neither this man sinned nor his parents, but regardless, God's works might be revealed with him." The "works of God" in the Gospel of John are consistently connected to belief. In this man will be another believer, another disciple. At the end of the story, the formerly blind man worships Jesus, recognizing Jesus as the source of his healing. Only God can heal on the sabbath.

"Who sinned?" is an ableist question. Our institutions privilege abled persons. What aspects of our corporate lives regularly discriminate against persons with disabilities through lack of access? How have we, without consciousness and with complacency, participated in normate society? The encounter with the Pharisees culminates in the expulsion of the formerly blind man—he is "thrown out" (*ekballō*), the word most frequently used for casting out demons. "Demonizing those who refuse to cooperate with the hegemonic systems is common . . . and is a general claim even today about PWDs [persons with a disability]."[38]

From the perspective of disability studies, "who sinned?" also exposes the forces of imperial power, where disabled bodies were "sites of imperial incursions and contest."[39] "John's disabled bodies show that the imperial world is not healed and that imperial power is not a force for wholeness as imperial self-presentation claims. To the contrary, imperial power is death-bringing, paralyzing, sickening, blinding. It paralyzes with disabling power, blinding its subjects so that they cannot see a different world. It is self-deceiving. Jesus' healing interventions effect the life, wholeness, and insight that imperial elites boast of but cannot deliver."[40] From this perspective, Jesus' healings address the hurt and harm of empire.[41]

A particular challenge for interpreting this passage is Johannine theology. The dualism characteristic of the Gospel of John exacerbates harmful readings of the healing of the man born blind when blindness is equated with darkness. Blindness was a "common literary topos in antiquity,"[42] with blindness representing ignorance. Recognizing that John might be using this topos is helpful to some extent, but how John explicates light/darkness and how the passage lands on actual blind bodies require critical attention. Light/darkness is a dominant symbolic framework for John's theology, introduced in the prologue, "The light shines in the darkness, and the darkness did not overcome it" (1:5). John links the incarnation, the Word becoming flesh, with light and with the goodness of light as expressed in the creation story of Genesis. "Let there be light" is God's command that overcomes the darkness of the world. There is no doubt that the author of John uses the creation story to build the light/dark symbolism of the Fourth Gospel.

Throughout the narrative, the references to times of the day indicate the status of a person's relationship with Jesus. Thus, Nicodemus visits Jesus at night (3:2), a brief encounter that ends in only confusion and misunderstanding for Nicodemus, "How can these things be?" (v. 9). When Jesus meets the Samaritan woman at Jacob's well outside the Samaritan city of Sychar, the time is noon—the lightest and brightest time of the day—and the conversation between her and Jesus results in her witness to her townspeople. "And it was night" (13:30) is the time reference that marks the betrayal of Judas.

Given this symbolic framework, it is difficult to avoid linking blindness with darkness, and the blind man becomes a "narrative prosthesis." "There are two ways in which a disabled character can serve as a prosthetic for the narrative: first as a *narrative element* that somehow resolves the problem of deviance; second, as a metaphorical device drawing on physiognomic reasoning."[43] In the case of the man born blind, he is a double crutch, if you will. His condition is observed and needs an explanation, which then sets in motion the rehabilitation; his blindness serves as the metaphorical template for the Pharisees' spiritual blindness at the end of the chapter.

There needs to be caution with readings that skip quickly to the metaphorical meaning of the man's blindness. The Gospel of John is its own worst enemy in this regard by creating this powerful metaphorical backdrop. This then demands hermeneutical dexterity on the part of the interpreter, not "to buy into John's symbolic universe wholesale, without realizing the implications it may have for understandings of disability and the danger of stigmatizing people with disabilities in the process."[44] Bringing the term "narrative prosthetic" into play, we begin to realize our own tendencies to make sense of illness, making the man a mere pawn in a spiritual story. We must use abundant caution in our readings, so that we are not thus making these persons "invisible" or exacerbating their suffering.[45]

Like the miraculous healing in John 5, the healing of the man born blind in John 9 is brief, only two verses long. Jesus makes some mud, spreads it on the man's eyes, and tells him to go and wash in the pool of Siloam. The blind man obeys this unknown voice and returns being able to see for the first time in his life. But this story of a formerly blind man does not end once he is cured. The rest of the chapter and into chapter 10 narrates what having sight means for the formerly blind man who never asked to be cured in the first place. The narrative space given to the subsequent conversations and then Jesus' own interpretation of the healing communicates that more important than gaining his sight is what difference this makes for his life going forward. As a result, "it is the characterization of the man born blind more than anything else that makes John 9 a particularly useful story for reflecting on human disability and the service of God."[46]

In the opening scene, it is also important to note that the blind man does not ask to be cured. It is an abled perspective that assumes persons with disabilities desire a cure. It is the normate assumption that the man's blindness is something that needs to be overcome. As Solevåg notes, "Within the disability movement . . . people with disabilities are often more comfortable with their nonnormative bodies and less interested in cure than able-bodied people tend to assume."[47] Jesus sees the man born blind and takes the initiative to restore his sight.

Jesus also knows that to cure the man of his blindness is only the beginning. The point of the miracle is not the miracle but the relationship to which it will lead. The future for the man born blind will be bound up in being a part of a new community, and perhaps, a community he has never had. We have been told that the man spends the better part of his days begging (9:8), likely having little to no social, companionable, or even physical contact with others. Persons with disabilities would experience various levels of marginalization, depending on the nature of their impairment. We do not know the extent of the man's support, or lack thereof. The story does introduce neighbors and the man's parents, with the parents' reluctance a stark contrast to the blind man's confidence.[48] We can assume, however, a certain level of ostracization from having to beg for survival. In this regard, "disabled bodies in John's Gospel are signs and sites of the assertion and negotiation of imperial power. These bodies reveal the lie of imperial claims to be a force for wholeness and healing."[49]

A careful reading of the story through the lens of a disability hermeneutic reveals that the man is not merely identified as the blind man or the formerly blind man. Other designations underline his "status as a human being."[50] He is referred to as a man/human being (9:1, 24, 30); by different pronouns; as "son," and as "beggar." Moreover, he is the only character in the Gospel of John besides Jesus to identify himself as "I am." As questions are asked about his identity, the man speaks up. "Some were saying, 'It is he.' Others were saying, 'No, but it is someone like him.' He kept saying, 'I am the man'" (v. 9). While a number of translations add the pronoun "he" or "the man" after "I am," there is no predicate nominative in the Greek text. "The man's insistence that he is the same man they once knew . . . from his perspective, his disability was never his defining characteristic; he knows himself to be the same person, blind or sighted."[51]

Before the man is thrown out of his synagogue community by the religious leaders (v. 34), he argues with them, defends himself, and ends up speaking the truth about Jesus' identity, "If this man were not from God, he could do nothing" (v. 33). While English translations intimate uncertainty in the man's statement, the Greek syntax is a false condition, better translated, "If this man were not from God—but he is—he could do nothing—but he can do anything!" The man embodies agency, not one simply to be fixed. He is "not only a broken figure in need of compassion and healing but as a person in his own right. We are able to get to know him as a thoughtful, brave, amusing, but above all, ordinary person."[52]

In Solevåg's analysis of the healings in John 5 and John 9, she notes that the majority of interpretations tend to have a more positive assessment of the blind man than of the healed man in John 5. Read in light of one another, "the 'weak' man signifies partial understanding, whereas the blind man represents faith in Jesus."[53] In this physiognomic move, where outer appearance is linked to inner morality[54] and which "diverts attention from literal disability to questions of inner character,"[55] the lame man in John 5 is viewed negatively by a connection to three specific details. First, the man is cast in a deleterious light because he seems less than enthusiastic in his response to Jesus' question, "Do you want to be made well?" (5:6). Second, compared to the man born blind (9:35–38), the man in John 5 does not express proper gratitude to Jesus for his healing. Third, the man is assumed to have ratted out Jesus to the authorities: "The man went away and told the Jews that it was Jesus who had made him well. Therefore, the Jews started persecuting Jesus, because he was doing such things on the sabbath" (vv. 15–16). Jesus had disappeared into the crowd after the healing, later finding the man in the temple. From an exegetical or narrative point of view, the man's response can be interpreted as positive. Jesus finds him in the temple because the man has realized that only God could be the source of his being cured. Since Jesus had absconded after the healing, the man is found in the temple worshiping God. The man's going to the authorities to name his healer could be an act of bravery, even witness. Like the Samaritan woman in John 4, who courageously returns to her townspeople and tells them of her encounter with Jesus, the man in John 5 risks further interrogation, perhaps even a charge of collusion, by telling the authorities the identity of his healer. From the point of view of a disability hermeneutic, the unflattering assessment of the man in John 5 is a situation where the "interpreters have conflated the man's illness with his personality and understand him as weak in character as well as in body."[56] It is ableist presumptions that blame the man for his supposed dearth of zeal for wanting to be healed.

When a sighted perspective is left unchallenged, the only means of salvation for the man in chapter 9 is being healed of his blindness. Yong notes counterarguments to ableist presuppositions.[57] First, the light/darkness dualism in the Gospel does not have to result in a negative assessment of the blind man. As Yong notes, blind persons are capable of appreciating "how such metaphors work without being offended by them."[58] Second, the formerly blind man ends up becoming a disciple and worshiper of Jesus, one of Jesus' sheep even, when the Shepherd Discourse (10:1–18) is taken into account as Jesus' interpretation of the healing. It is not his physical healing that makes him a disciple but his eventual spiritual sight that recognizes who Jesus is. Comparatively, the Pharisees, while they can see physically, are unable to perceive Jesus' identity. The blind man progresses in his spiritual sight, from seeing Jesus as "the man called Jesus" (9:11), to "a prophet" (v. 17), to "from God" (v. 33), to "Lord" (v. 38). John 9 is the longest absence of Jesus in the entire Gospel, and unlike any other healing narrative, "it is the events that unfold while he is 'off-stage' that are the most significant."[59] The spiritual sight of the formerly blind man grows in Jesus' absence, deemphasizing the need for Jesus' actual presence to be able to see. One does not have to see Jesus to see who he is. It is not necessary, therefore, to have one's sight restored to become aware of Jesus' identity, even to become a disciple. In the end, the man is less focused on his healing than on his own realization of his "sight" compared to the lack of sight of the Pharisees.[60] He tells them, "Here is an astonishing thing! You do not know where he comes from, and yet he opened my eyes. We know that God does not listen to sinners, but he does listen to one who worships him and obeys his will. Never since the world began has it been heard that anyone opened the eyes of a person born blind. If this man were not from God, he could do nothing" (vv. 30–33). The real miracle of this story is the man's ability to comprehend Jesus' true identity—Jesus comes from God.

Bringing a disability hermeneutic to John 9 allows for critical differentiation between ableist presumptions and a text's own theological commitments. "It is sighted presuppositions, not the text itself, that canonized God in terms of light and sightedness, thus condemning darkness and blindness as blots within the created order that must finally be eliminated."[61] Of course, a less generous read would conclude that blindness and darkness are exclusionary, without hopes of rescuing the text from its own worldview. One's interpretive stance must always come under scrutiny when it comes to impulses either to save or to condemn the text. For some, texts of this nature are unredeemable and can only function to marginalize further.

A myopic focus on sight alone also betrays a sighted perspective. "Seeing is believing" is often connected with John 9 and then, later in the Gospel, with Thomas (20:25). The larger narrative context, however, suggests that this is indeed a limiting interpretation. The man in chapter 9 first *hears* Jesus before he *sees* Jesus. Reading forward into chapter 10 and Jesus' discourse concerning the sign, hearing becomes more prominent. The sheep know the voice of the shepherd and will run from the stranger whose voice they do not know. The concluding verses of the whole narrative unit (10:19–21) also emphasize the importance of hearing, "Many of them were saying, 'He has a demon and is out of his mind. Why listen to him?'" (v. 20), bringing the story of the healing of the blind man full circle.

Read from a hermeneutic of disability, the wider theological theme of the incarnation in the Gospel of John points to emphasis on the body. Clark-Soles identifies four key perspectives that undergird a disability hermeneutic.[62] First, God, the divine, is embodied in the Word made flesh. God entered into the fullness of human form, so that the body itself is divine. Second, the Word made flesh leads to an emphasis on intimacy, where bodies take center stage in the telling of the narrative. Third, the Fourth Gospel is exceedingly sensual—all of the senses play a part in encounters of the Word dwelling among us. Finally, "bodies do not need to be overcome"[63] but are sites of experiences of the Word made flesh. The man born blind "is not presented merely as a stock character representing faith in Jesus. Neither is he portrayed as a victim deserving of pity (recall that he does not request healing). Rather, the story depicts a real person involved in a deliberative process about a personal experience, a process that is expressed through conversation with the religious authorities. Thus, the story is not so much about what Jesus did but what the man is doing."[64] The incarnational thrust of John's Gospel means that the man born blind says to us, "I am not a metaphor."[65]

HOMILETICAL IMPLICATIONS

Preaching stories that have characters who are disabled demand homiletical dexterity. Like other minoritized groups, persons with a disability can easily be restigmatized by our unconscious and unchecked biases. Our interpretations can be harmful, and even incorrect, if we are unaware of how disability is functioning in a particular narrative. As discussed above, it is essential to understand how blindness works as a metaphor in John 9, particularly as connected to the symbolism of light and darkness in John's Gospel. "How disability is used in a narrative is helpful in order both to reveal biases of earlier interpretations and to suggest alternative readings."[66] Having the vocabulary of a disability hermeneutic enables the preacher to name ableist interpretations. In the case of John 9, those interpretations that might perpetuate a prosthetic narrative scheme will conclude that the blind man is dispensable. Yet, reading into chapter 10, we learn that the blind man is not expendable, because he heard Jesus' voice, followed him, and is now a sheep of Jesus' fold (v. 16). A disability hermeneutic functions to correct "symbolic or spiritualized readings" that "render the disabled figures invisible" and the ways in which we have engaged in interpretive methods that "invisibilize" disabled bodies.[67] Sometimes those who think of themselves as "normal" are really the ones in need of healing. "As long as our primary perception of ourselves is as persons who can see, or hear, or walk, or think rationally over against those who cannot do these things, our sin of stereotyping and exclusion remains."[68]

Sometimes we are called to read against the text for the sake of preaching the good news. "The problematic sides of [the Bible's] representations of disability and their ensuing theologies need to be exposed."[69] While an awareness of a disability hermeneutic will result in more responsible, even more ethical, preaching, the preacher will still have to navigate the theological waters that get stirred up by our human desire for understanding and explanation, especially when it comes to illness. The human condition always wants to know why—and more often than not, that "why" is directed to God. Regardless of our capacity to acknowledge that God does not cause impairment, we cannot help but make that connection at some point. Rather than pretend that the "why" question does not get asked, perhaps the preacher articulates the deep-seated fear that, somehow or in some way, an impairment of any kind means that we have wronged God.

A disability hermeneutic brought to the story of the healing of the man born blind exposes our current but likely unspoken theological assumption that illness, disease, disability, and the like could be the result of, or punishment for, our sin.[70] We somehow deserve this malady, having done something wrong that warrants God's wrath. While logically we know this is not the case, when we are trying to understand or make sense of calamity, rationales are rarely logical. We, or the impaired person, merit the infirmity. So much of how we view health and well-being is caught up in our faith structures. We pray for healing and struggle theologically when the outcome for which we prayed does not come to pass. As a result, bringing a disability lens to our interpretation of the Bible, especially in our meaning making for proclamation, will then surface buried levels of our beliefs. The preacher needs to be ready pastorally for this unearthing.

Another key homiletical implication of a hermeneutic of disability is to ask how the church contributes to rhetoric around disability. In our sermons, do our stories or illustrations include persons with disabilities? Do persons with disabilities hear themselves in our sermons? Or are they further marginalized by sermons that preach only to a certain demographic? All preachers are guilty of narrow illustrative imagination; our sermon stories are often geared to the proverbial eighteen- to thirty-four-year-olds, or to people like us. What kind of voice has the church had when it comes to society's response to and for persons with disability? Is the church perceived as a leader in anti-ableist work? Or has the church been silent, skirting responsibility for its own complicity in ableism? How and where does the church advocate for disabled persons—insisting that the kingdom of God is not fully realized without such members? In other words, having a disability perspective should raise ecclesial questions: What is church? What should church look like? "Who is missing?"[71] Are we truly church when we deflect accountability?

A disability approach also demands reevaluation of church practices. Such evaluation not only necessitates assessment of church or building accessibility, but also has significant ramifications for ritual. The Lord's Supper and baptisms are likely spaces and places where persons with disabilities most experience otherness. Preaching is not limited to the spoken Word dedicated as the sermon on Sunday morning. We preach the good news—God's presence among us—in the entirety of our worship experiences. Our rituals are theological claims—they say something about God's activity in the world. When our rituals exclude or set up barriers for persons with disabilities, we not only prevent connection with God in a particular way, we also communicate that God has limitations in gaining access to those God loves. These questions of worship, discipleship, and vocation then lead to the question, who gets to participate?[72] A disability hermeneutic thus raises the larger theological issue of hospitality. "With each denial of hospitality, we calcify the sin of dehumanization."[73]

A hermeneutic of disability invites critical reflection on how we imagine God. Imagining God is often, of course, an exercise of looking in the mirror. We see God the way we want to see ourselves, and vice versa. Like it or not, we form God in our own image. Do we ever picture God as disabled? What does it sound like for persons with disabilities to hear, "You were made in the image of God"? How do we recognize and name "false understandings"[74] of God that then lead to questions about worthiness, about being loved: "What did I do to deserve this fate? Does God love me?" If a person could be considered a mistake, then what does this say about God's sovereignty?[75] The attributes we ascribe to God have everything to do with how we talk about and view disability.[76] "To denigrate differently abled bodies is to denigrate creation and, by extension, its creator."[77] The Fourth Evangelist connects the presence of the Word back to the creation of the world. As "everything came into being" through Jesus, is not then everything and everyone "good"? Thus, "'good bodies' come in a variety of forms. Rather than 'fixing' bodies that deviate from the 'norm,' the concern should be to fix society to make it inclusive of all bodies."[78]

Finally, a disability hermeneutic is a critical conversation partner for the sake of resurrection preaching. The Christian belief about the resurrection of the body raised numerous debates in early Christian discourse about the exact nature of the resurrected body. The healing stories in the Gospels were "proof texts" for resurrected perfect bodies, abled and without blemish. Yet the resurrection appearances of

Jesus describe Jesus' body as still having the marks of crucifixion (Luke 24:39–40; John 20:25–27). "Jesus's resurrection body is not a perfectly able body but one bearing the marks of a lived life as the primary signs of his identity and thus the proof of continuity."[79] What if the crucified and resurrected Jesus Christ, with wounds, was the disabled God?[80]

> Resurrection is not about the negation or erasure of our disabled bodies in hopes of perfect images, untouched by physical disability; rather Christ's resurrection offers hope that our nonconventional, and sometimes difficult, bodies participate fully in the imago Dei and that God whose nature is love and who is on the side of justice and solidarity is touched by our experience. God is changed by the experience of being a disabled body. This is what the Christian hope of resurrection means.[81]

FURTHER RESOURCES FOR PREACHING

Black, Kathy. *A Healing Homiletic: Preaching and Disability.* Nashville: Abingdon Press, 1996.

Kenny, Amy. *My Body Is Not a Prayer Request: Disability Justice in the Church.* Grand Rapids: Brazos Press, 2022.

9

The Bible and Trauma Theory

INTRODUCTION

"The phenomenon of trauma is not new. There is no time in history when we can say that trauma began."[1] Only in the span of a century, however, have trauma studies and trauma theory been formalized, first as study concentrated on individually experienced trauma, but now expanded into historical trauma, institutional trauma, collective trauma, and global trauma.

When trauma becomes a dedicated lens through which to view the world, we recognize that trauma is everywhere. It is a fact of life. Traumatic life events are individual: sexual assault and domestic abuse, tragic deaths, a veteran's experience of war. Traumatic life events are communal: 9/11, Sandy Hook, the murder of George Floyd. Trauma theory, trauma studies, also attend to the testimony, the survival literature, born out of catastrophic events, particularly of the twentieth century: the Holocaust, the bombings of Hiroshima and Nagasaki, the Vietnam War.[2] In the 1970s, psychology began to identify "traumatic stress" and trauma as "a distinct type of suffering that overwhelms a person's normal capacity to cope."[3] Trauma literature defies categorization and "transcends genre," taking on multiple literary forms to witness to the trauma recalled.[4]

Regardless of the specified trauma, trauma studies "focuses on the ways in which an overwhelming event or events of violence continue in the present, returning and impacting the present and the future in unaccounted-for ways."[5] Said another way, "While the initial experience is 'missed,' not fully integrated into the psyche of the victim, the experience perpetuates itself through recurrent manifestations of memory of the event."[6] Or, to put it simply, "Trauma is what does not go away"[7] and is "overwhelming, unbelievable, and unbearable."[8] It is life lived in the residual, the remaining, with the primary persisting truth being that life is "continually marked by the ongoingness of death";[9] life and death are no longer linear but indissolubly linked. Life now means something radically different because "there is no access to life as it was before the storm."[10] Trauma disarranges reality itself, and trauma survivors are forced to cope with a "dual reality: the reality of a relatively secure and predictable present that lives side by side with a ruinous, ever-present past."[11] Trauma also disrupts "the integration of memories, the ability to create coherent personal narratives, the establishment of healthy relationships, and the ability to construct life-giving visions for the future."[12] The word "trauma" comes from the Greek word meaning a wound or a physical injury caused by violence. "To be traumatized is to be slashed or struck down by a hostile external force that threatens to destroy you."[13] In trauma theory, the initial trauma is the "historical experience of the wound."[14] In this regard, trauma theory recognizes the effects of trauma on the entire body. Addressing trauma is not simply a psychological exercise, but care for and healing for the whole person.[15]

Addressing the "ongoing realities of a death that does not go away" is a key component of trauma theory. Trauma, therefore, is also defined as "an encounter with death." This encounter with death, however, does not have to be a literal death but becomes a means by which to signify the effect of trauma in and on one's life. All that one has known about life and the world and how to navigate life and the world is devastated in the traumatic event. This disruption and disorientation are the nature of survival after trauma and hold an expected complexity in the convergence of psychology, sociology, epistemology, "constructions of the self," and theology. Shelly Rambo describes this survival as the "'middle'—the figurative site in which death and life are no longer bounded."[16]

While it may seem obvious, trauma theory names the pervasiveness of trauma. There is both "primary traumatization," which "affects those who witness a traumatic event or have a traumatic response to a direct personal experience," and "secondary" or "indirect traumatization," in which persons are "traumatized by the traumatic experience of some-one else."[17] Traumatic events are traumatic in that they pose the "threat of annihilation."[18]

SUMMARY OF THE APPROACH

As a contextual approach to reading biblical texts, trauma theory entered into dialogue with biblical interpretation in the early 2000s, primarily through studies of exilic texts. The survival and aftermath of the destruction of Jerusalem in 586 BCE and the Babylonian captivity gave rise to literature that spoke into and out of this collective traumatic experience. While exilic material is an obvious entry point for yoking trauma studies and biblical interpretation, "much of the Hebrew Bible is written in response to trauma: the Assyrian onslaught against Israel in the eighth century BCE, the Babylonian destruction of Jerusalem and the subsequent exile at the end of the sixth century BCE, the persecutions under Greek rule in the second century BCE."[19]

The Bible is replete with stories that narrate traumatic experiences; the flood, the rejection of Hagar and Ishmael, the rapes of Dinah and Tamar, and the Psalmic laments are but a few examples that "could be explored in light of traumatic testimony."[20] In the New Testament, Paul's experience of the resurrected Christ on the Damascus road was, in his words, an apocalypse (Gal. 1:12), upending life as Paul knew it. The Christ event is "inaccessible, in its totality, to the mind. It continually returns as a resistance to meaning, to ritual, to language. The Christ event returns as a force that continually disrupts our usual forms of remembering and ritualizing."[21] The passion narratives, the healing stories, the persecution that the book of Revelation assumes, and the Gospels' postdestruction of the Second Temple in 70 CE perspective all have the potential for greater insight from the perspective of trauma. We might also affirm that "the central narrative of the Christian faith is one of trauma and grace" as even "Jesus's life begins in trauma—for how else can we imagine a birth for a young girl far from home?"[22]

Scholarship that brings trauma theory into dialogue with biblical interpretation is clear in noting that such efforts do not represent a defined method of interpretation but a "frame of reference that . . . can yield interesting results in the study of the biblical literature and the communities that produced it."[23] In other words, for biblical scholars, "trauma hermeneutics is used to interpret texts in their historical contexts and as a means of exploring the appropriation of texts, in contexts both past and present."[24] In particular, three areas of emphasis inform biblical trauma hermeneutics: psychology, sociology, and literary and cultural studies. "Psychology contributes to our understanding of the effects of trauma on individuals and on those processes that facilitate survival, recovery, and resilience. Sociology provides insights into collective dimensions of traumatic experience. Literary and cultural studies open pathways for exploring the role and function of texts as they encode and give witness to traumatic suffering and construct discursive and aesthetic spaces for fostering recovery and resilience."[25] Biblical scholars, therefore, employ these various approaches in their interpretations of texts, and these areas of focus overlap in how they might influence a specific trauma hermeneutic.[26] Trauma theory provides a framework for biblical interpretation that "allows trauma in the text and in our world to come to light. Biblical scholars pay attention to violence, oppression, exile, and the ways that these affect the individual and community. They pay attention to the ways that individuals and communities are traumatized, as well as the mechanisms for survival and resiliency."[27]

At the same time, wrestling with survival, suffering, and theodicy has always been necessary for persons who lodge trust in the God of what is now known as the Bible, both the persons in the texts and the persons who read those texts. "Trauma has a profound impact on our capacity to trust God."[28] A central component of trauma theory as it relates to biblical studies is theodicy, "the theological discourse" and "theoretical practice of reconciling claims about the goodness of God with the presence of evil in the world."[29] Trauma introduces distinct elements of suffering that press theology to expand its ways of construction. Trauma defies explanation and systemization, while theology often leans toward both. Biblical interpretation through the lens of trauma, therefore, is not a move toward solution or resolution. Rather, a trauma perspective allows for insight into the human condition as narrated in the Bible and as experienced by persons of faith reading the Bible.

SAMPLE TEXT: JOHN 20:1–18

Since "constructing a trauma narrative is an act of meaning-making,"[30] viewing the resurrection narratives through this perspective uniquely encapsulates their inherent hopes. Before the triumphalism that tends to seep into interpretations of the resurrection appearances, there should be, because there is present, attention to trauma. As noted above, the passion narratives can be understood as trauma literature. The Gospel writers were uniquely tasked with making some kind of sense out of a long-expected Messiah who was hung on a tree, "for anyone hung on a tree is under God's curse" (Deut. 21:23). Jesus' crucifixion was a trauma on multiple levels. "It is a shared sense of suffering felt by the collective that motivates certain groups to propose narratives to name and account for the suffering and that also moves the collective to accept a given narrative."[31] The Gospel writers were not simply recording the events of Jesus' arrest, trial, torture, and punishment; because of their communities and for the sake of their communities, they composed narratives to assist in a kind of meaning making that seemed almost impossible. This is also true of the resurrection appearances.[32] They are not quick fixes or included in the Gospels to gloss over the loss and suffering—the trauma—of the crucifixion. Read through the lens of trauma, the resurrection appearances are poignant convergences of the levels of trauma laid out in trauma theory.

Before a close examination of Jesus' appearance to Mary Magdalene in the garden, however, any discussion of intersections between trauma theory and the Fourth Gospel needs to be aware of the trauma of the community to which the Fourth Evangelist was writing. A majority of scholars argue that the Johannine community was cast out of its synagogue (*aposynagōgos*; John 9:22; 12:42; 16:2) for professing a belief in Jesus. In John 9:22, the parents of the man born blind fear this fate if they speak up in support of their son's healing. In 12:42, Jesus' last public discourse before the events of the hour, many people do believe in Jesus, even some of the religious authorities, "but because of the Pharisees they did not confess it, for fear that they would be put out of the synagogue." In 16:2, Jesus is clear about the disciples' fate, "They will put you out of the synagogues. Indeed, an hour is coming when those who kill you will think that by doing so they are offering worship to God." The Johannine community experienced a death of exponential proportions. To be cast out of the synagogue community meant potentially permanent separation from or abandonment by family members, social systems, communal infrastructures, and religious life. In many respects, without the parameters in place for worship, it was also a separation from God.

The Fourth Gospel, therefore, is often considered sectarian literature, as the community had to reimagine and justify its identity. The dualism, the insider/outsider language, the concept of judgment are all characteristic of a sectarian mind-set and literature. Less discussed in scholarship, however, is the trauma that this community would have experienced—psychologically, socially, and communally. A trauma hermeneutic, therefore, offers an important perspective—even corrective—to what is often mistakenly viewed as a closed-off and excluded community. To what extent does the Johannine symbolic world give witness to themes of survival and resilience?

In recognizing this first trauma of the Johannine community, the trauma of the resurrection narratives in the Fourth Gospel becomes all the more acute. The Johannine community is grappling with trauma upon trauma, giving witness to what life now means "in the aftermath of death."[33] Rambo argues that witness, therefore, takes on a vital role in trauma as "the hinge linking the shattering and rethinking, the undoing and the regeneration," between death and life. Witness, therefore, "is defined by its positioning" and is thus a "middle activity."[34] In "witnessing from the middle," therefore, "first, a person is positioned in respect to suffering in such a way that she can see truths that often escape articulation, that emerge through cracks in the dominant logic. Second, this tenuous placement also means that the witness is subject to the continual elisions that make it impossible to see, hear, or touch clearly."[35]

This perspective on witness and trauma sheds light on this central embodiment of discipleship in the Gospel of John. Witnessing to the revelation of God in Jesus is the called-for response to an encounter with the I AM. The Fourth Evangelist portrays John the Baptist as the first example of such witness (1:6–8), and the verb is used more than thirty times in the Gospel. The Holy Spirit witnesses about Jesus (15:26) and the disciples are called to give testimony about Jesus (v. 27). To witness is a fitting discipleship corollary to the theological claim of the Fourth Gospel—the Word became flesh. The world as we have known it can no longer be. The atemporal has become temporal. The dead will not stay dead.

In the story of Mary Magdalene in John 20,[36] there are a number of details that, through a trauma perspective, both give new insights into the interpretation of this well-known story and resituate how we locate the resurrection in our overall belief systems. While Mary Magdalene is the first noted witness to the resurrection, she does not "simply receive and pass on the news of Jesus' death."[37] Indeed, through the lens of trauma, she can't. "Her witness reflects the complexities of seeing in the after of death."[38]

We first need to recall that Mary Magdalene's trauma is a kind of double trauma. As one of the disciples at the foot of the cross, along with Jesus' mother, her sister, Mary the wife of Clopas, and the Beloved Disciple, Mary Magdalene has already witnessed Jesus' death.[39] She saw his body hanging on the cross. She heard him speak his last words. She felt his last breath as he gave up his spirit. Mary Magdalene carries this first traumatic event with her as she makes her way, alone, in the dark, to the garden. We do not know why she goes to Jesus' tomb, except that in John, she does not witness the burial of Jesus, as she does in Matthew, Mark, and Luke.[40] Jesus has already been anointed for burial and laid in the tomb by Joseph of Arimathea and Nicodemus, so there is no need for her to bring spices for his anointing. Now in John 20:1, she goes to the tomb expecting to find it closed with Jesus' body inside. Instead, the stone has been rolled away. While she does not look in the tomb yet, her immediate assumption is that the body has been stolen. Why else would the stone be moved? Herein lies the double trauma of the moment. She has already witnessed Jesus' death and now she fears that his body has again been violated.

Why does Mary Magdalene visit the tomb? Why do we visit the graves of our loved ones? The funeral or memorial service is over. The interment has already happened. There is nothing more left to do but to start to grieve. It is also important to note that in John, she is completely alone. There are no companions with her, as there are in Matthew, Mark, and Luke. She goes to the tomb empty-handed and empty-hearted.

According to Rambo, Mary Magdalene's capacity to witness is obstructed by three details: the darkness, her tears, and her restricted view inside the tomb. The story is told in a way that represents the confusion of this middle of which she is trying to make sense.[41] At first, Mary sees only that the stone has been rolled away and, unlike Peter and the Beloved Disciple, Mary never actually enters the tomb, but looks into or stoops down to it. While the darkness would have likely impaired Mary's vision, it also has symbolic significance in the Gospel of John, intensifying the drama and trauma of the moment. In the Gospel of John, darkness is a connection to unbelief or represents severing one's relationship with God/Jesus. The symbolic referents of light/darkness were already set out in the prologue to the Gospel, where the incarnation, the Word made flesh, is first described as the light shining in the darkness (1:5). Once this symbolic world is established, the Fourth Evangelist need only include the detail of the time of day to indicate the status of one's relationship to Jesus.[42] For example, Judas betrays Jesus by abandoning the relationship he has had with Jesus. After having his feet washed by Jesus and sharing a meal with his fellow disciples, he exits the room, "and it was night" (13:30). In the case of Mary Magdalene, she has not abandoned her relationship with Jesus, but she likely wonders if Jesus has. The darkness indicates that the light of the world—Jesus—is not present. The light has been extinguished. For Mary, her relationship with Jesus is broken.

There are four references to Mary Magdalene's weeping in the garden (20:11, twice; 20:13, 15). Through the perspective of trauma and Rambo's metaphor of witnessing from the middle, Mary's tears point to her "unseeing" witness, characteristic of response to trauma. This does not question the validity of her witness but rather acknowledges the inability to make sense of what she is seeing. "She points to a different kind of presence, whose form cannot be readily identified or can only be received through multiple experiences of misrecognitions. She encounters not simply the absence of Jesus, but a mixed terrain of his absence and presence."[43] Mary's weeping recalls the raising of Lazarus, the only other death narrated in the Gospel of John. Twice in the narrative of the raising of Lazarus, the verb *klaiō* (weep) is used, indicating the trauma of the event: "The Jews who were with her in the house, consoling her, saw Mary get up quickly and go out. They followed her because they thought that she was going to the tomb to weep there" (11:31). "When Jesus saw her weeping, and the Jews who came with her also weeping, he was greatly disturbed in spirit and deeply moved" (v. 33).[44]

In the story of the raising of Lazarus, Jesus' response to Mary's weeping intimates his own distress. Jesus is moved and his spirit is deeply troubled. And then, Jesus himself weeps (v. 35). The verb used for Jesus' weeping (*dakryō*) is not the same as the one for Mary and her friends in John 11 and for Mary Magdalene in John 20, but is used only here in the entire New Testament. This is an unprecedented moment—a traumatic moment. The narrative space given to the trauma, grief, death, and raising of Lazarus is brought forward to this moment in the garden. Chapter 11 in John's Gospel is frequently titled "The Raising of Lazarus," somewhat of a misnomer. Lazarus's exiting the tomb is summarized in only two verses, "When [Jesus] had said this, he cried with a loud voice, 'Lazarus, come out!' The dead man came out, his hands and feet bound with strips of cloth, and his face wrapped in a cloth. Jesus said to them, 'Unbind him, and let him go'" (vv. 43–44). The narrative emphasis is on grief and trauma.

When we arrive at the garden with Mary Magdalene in John 20, the same kind of literary space is devoted to the grief and trauma of her moment. Paying attention to Mary's encounter with Jesus through the lens of trauma brings to the surface the disorientation and overwhelmingness of the moment. Trauma "outstrips our capacity to cope, our sense of agency, and overwhelms our meaning-making capacity," even outweighing "the power of imagination."[45] Mary's inability to recognize Jesus clues us in to the confusion that the trauma evokes, as "much of what she is witnessing is inaccessible to her."[46] At the same time, the delayed recognition intensifies the trauma, just as the delayed telling of the raising of Lazarus intensifies the grief surrounding Lazarus's death.

Read through the lens of trauma, this narrative technique of delayed response and recognition generates three interpretive results. First, the author of the Fourth Gospel places the reader in the same position as the characters in the story. As we hear a story meant not just for the immediate audience, but also for future readers (John 20:30–31), we find ourselves caught up in Mary's confusion, Mary's grief, and Mary's trauma. We are there with her, alongside her, feeling her feelings, crying her tears. The narrative suspense—when will she recognize Jesus?—puts us there. We too are faced with the trauma of the crucifixion and the empty tomb, an interpretive space that calls forth reinterpretation of the resurrection appearances. The resurrection stories cannot, and do not intend to, erase the trauma of the passion narrative. Reading these stories through the lens of trauma attends to these "indirect encounters" with what we "do not fully comprehend of the event."[47]

When narrative space is given to these expressions of sorrow, the story communicates that grief is acceptable, in fact, expected. One of the important contributions of trauma theory is to take back the idea that trauma is something from which someone needs to "move on." The fact that Scripture creates room for response to trauma then affirms that need in our own lives. These moments in Scripture are not just theologized encapsulations of witnessed events but lived experiences being textualized. In our efforts to make meaning from biblical texts, we want answers or solutions or something "that will preach." Our engagement with the biblical texts is all too often for the sake of argument or apology. The resurrection appearance to Mary coupled with a trauma perspective helps us imagine the ways these stories are mirrors through which to view our own lives, especially traumatic events.

The deferred moment of realization for Mary acknowledges that her trauma is real—and so is she. As critical and central as her witness is, and will be, it is allowed an interim for holding its truth.[48] What she is experiencing is not graspable—it "escapes cognition."[49] To hold Mary Magdalene to a certain standard of correct testimony is to discount her very real reactions to a trauma recalled by an empty tomb. The inability of Mary to recognize Jesus is indicative of this trauma moment. The obstruction of her sight—because of the dark, her tears, and her position in relation to the tomb—then offers some explanation as to why she is unable to recognize Jesus. While much interpretive ink has been spilled over the appearance of Jesus' body, through the lens of trauma, the focus is placed on the open wound that is Mary's trauma; for Mary, "the boundaries and parameters of life and death no longer seem to hold, to provide meaning."[50]

The moment of recognition for Mary is not seeing Jesus but hearing her name called. After first hearing his voice, "Woman, why are you weeping? Whom are you looking for?" (20:15), Mary assumes that the man is the gardener, because the tomb (19:41–42) and the resurrection appearance are in a garden. Through a trauma hermeneutic, the setting—in a garden—can also intensify the trauma. It was at a garden, an intimate place where Jesus often met with his disciples, that he was arrested.[51] A safe space was violated. Mary's inability to recognize Jesus by sight suggests once again the confusion of this traumatic moment, but "the sound of her name breaks through the obstructions of sight."[52]

The moment of recognition is when she hears her name being called. Mary is truly a disciple, a sheep of Jesus' own fold. "He calls his own sheep by name and leads them out. When he has brought out all his own, he goes ahead of them, and the sheep follow him because they know his voice" (10:3–4). Her response, therefore, calling Jesus "Rabbouni," acknowledges both Jesus' identity and her own realization of her discipleship.[53] Through the lens of trauma, even though Mary is not yet able to comprehend this moment of death in the midst of life, this "mixed terrain" of Jesus' "absence and presence,"[54] the relationship that she thought was broken has been restored.[55] In this realization, her immediate response is to hold onto that which was lost, or to restore what she once knew, what she once had before the trauma event.

With a trauma perspective, Mary's reaction signifies the incomprehension of trauma's middle space—when life now has to be interpreted through death. Jesus' words, "Do not hold on to me" (20:17), affirm the astounding difficulty of this moment for Mary—and for us.[56] This exchange captures "the central dynamics of trauma—its overwhelming violence, the shutdown of adaptive processes, and its lack of integration."[57] The verb "hold" is in the present tense in Greek, meaning that Mary is indeed holding on to Jesus. Now that she recognizes Jesus, that Jesus has returned to her, how could she possibly let go? While she might know and remember his promises, she cannot imagine saying goodbye yet again.

Because of a trauma hermeneutic, Mary's witnessing words, "I have seen the Lord," can be heard in a different way. "A trauma survivor may or may not be able to bear witness to the events and experiences that caused the trauma in the first place. They benefit tremendously, however, when they are able to testify to their own experience with a compassionate and generous listener."[58] Jesus instructs her to announce the ascension, not the resurrection, and she gives witness to neither. Instead, she announces where she is in that moment. To testify to what seems incredulous is not only impossible, it cannot be expected given the dynamics of trauma. Her witness is not invalid or deficient but is true to the "remaining" of a traumatic event. What Mary has experienced "exceeds categories of comprehension . . . exceeds the human capacity to take in and process the external world."[59] She testifies to what she saw, her Lord, but cannot fully understand her vision—a more than fitting theological response to what John testifies. We are never asked to understand the Word made flesh—only to abide in the Truth.

HOMILETICAL IMPLICATIONS

"Trauma is in our sanctuary" and often "hidden in the deep recesses of the pews."[60] The homiletical implications of interpreting the Bible through the lens of trauma might begin with a reconsideration of pastoral care and theological tenderness, especially when trauma calls into question the presence of God's grace.[61] Preaching trauma evokes a heightened pastoral sensibility. "The exigencies of after-living require a hermeneutics that engages wounds. How does a community work through such losses?"[62] They need a preacher.

Seeing Scripture through trauma helps preachers get a sense of how a text might "land" on the real bodies in their care. Preachers are always attentive to what their congregation needs to hear, but becoming aware of how trauma works can bring attention to how congregations actually hear and experience biblical texts. Pastoral care is not limited to phone or video calls, hospital or home visits, or acute circumstances. Pastoral care happens in preaching, either directly or indirectly, when preachers sense that a text might trigger a trauma event. This sensitivity also means that the preacher might anticipate increased pastoral care needs or requests following the sermon, and then will have to determine how to acknowledge and to invite these meetings and conversations. Is the preacher willing to give the space for trauma in the sermon that the text seems to suggest? Is the preacher able to anticipate the places in the following week where trauma will need to be processed? In this regard, preachers will need to be aware of how stories might recall traumas. This pastoral sensitivity leads to an awareness that other texts might have similar traumatic effects, especially if left unpreached. That is, there are stories in Scripture that should not be read out loud if there is no sermon to follow up on the trauma that they could reactivate. For example, the "divorce text" (Mark 10:2–12) has the potential to cause unfaced grief and should not be read out loud in the assembly if the sermon will be based on another passage. "Some wounds do not go away. They remain invisible, operating below the surface of our lives. When and if these wounds surface, they are often unrecognizable and misunderstood."[63] A trauma hermeneutic reminds preachers of the pastoral role of shaping a true resurrection people, often antithetical to society's wishes. Our congregations are like the upper room, that place

> where wounds are touched, and where shame, grief, and anger are released. It is a place of tenderness and courage. The resurrection scene directly speaks to the affective formation of a community struggling with death and loss. The capacities cultivated there require attunement to truths that rarely come to the surface. Infused with breath, each turns to those gathered in the room. A collective forms in the after-living. To be awakened to these realities is not easy work, but the razors will continue to cut us from within until we find ways to release them. This community meets at the junctures of histories and discerns points of crossing, embodying new configurations of life.[64]

Tending a trauma hermeneutic is an ethical responsibility of preaching. To ignore the intersection of trauma in the Bible and trauma in our lives will only reiterate a growing unuttered belief—that the Bible is not relevant to and for my life. Biblical relevancy is related to how we read and interpret the Bible. One purpose of preaching is to help parishioners be better readers of the Bible. Faithful interpretation is not only about respecting the diverse voices of the books included in the Bible, but also listening for how the authors give voice to the human condition. The Bible is as much a book about us as it is about God. While people might want to read the Bible for answers to life, preaching shows that the Bible is about accompanying our lives. As noted above, texts become mirrors instead of objects of our manipulations. Through the lens of trauma, it is impossible to be bystanders in the stories. No human being is untouched by trauma in some form. How the biblical texts speak out of and into trauma invites a kind of engagement with Scripture that might lead to our own capacity to witness. Like Mary, we might imagine being able "to testify to a death event in and through which a different conception of life emerges—a picture not of victorious new life but of persistent witness to love's survival."[65]

When preachers ignore elements of trauma in biblical texts, they also communicate that God, that theology, has nothing to say, nothing to contribute, when it comes to living in and after trauma. How is trauma "untouched by the practices and teachings of the Christian faith"? When are the traumas of our lives met with only "theological silence"?[66] If that is the case, the Christian faith will gradually lose its voice in the public sphere, if it hasn't already. One might also question to what extent church decline is also a result of the church's inability to speak directly into trauma, particularly collective, national, and global trauma. It is essential to "reexamine our religious stories and pay attention to spaces that offer solace to those who live the aftereffects of . . . trauma."[67]

Acknowledging trauma in our preaching can also address collective sin—how the church, the Bible, and theology have been perpetrators of trauma. Trauma preaching leads to confession of sins, the sins of the church that have been colonialism and imperialism, racism and sexism, heternormativity and anti-Semitism, thereby inflicting trauma on entire populations of peoples.[68]

At the writing of this book, our world is still in the middle of a global pandemic—a collective trauma that will mark the twenty-first century in ways yet unforeseen. But before this global trauma, we have become increasingly aware of horrific events in world, each having its own traumatic impact. Following the COVID pandemic, the United States was traumatized yet again by the death of George Floyd and the overturning of *Roe v. Wade*. Preachers had to adapt radically—both in how to do worship and in how to preach. With this pandemic came the realization of how ill-equipped preachers were to preach into and about this global trauma.

This inability cannot be blamed on gaps in their theological education; theological education at its heart is about adaptation. We study a God, we believe in a God, who constantly adapts—from covenants, to kings, to Christ. For the Christian believer, the ultimate adaptation of God was God becoming a human being in the form of Jesus, and even then, Jesus had to adapt as a human being. We study Scripture as a library of books that gives testimony to God's adaptation, even how God adapted God's self in the many individual encounters recorded in the Bible. And we study Scripture so as to preach—to show how the living Word of God adapts, is constantly and consistently contextualized in the faithful individual and in the communities of the faithful.

This homiletical unpreparedness comes from a historical unwillingness to preach into and about trauma in the first place; because of our own traumas, because the "push to move beyond the event, to a new and pure place," is so very potent, and because "it is much easier to deny or cover up trauma than it is to bear witness to it."[69] Perhaps naming the prevalence of trauma is exactly what preachers need to do. "Preachers carry the stories of many: those known personally to us, as well as those that occupy the larger social space."[70] We also hold our own traumas, sometimes too close. As Sarah Travis notes, "preachers will benefit from a strong awareness of their own responses to trauma and their own personal triggers. As witnesses to the wider world, we may find ourselves just as traumatized by public events as those to whom we preach."[71] This is painful proclamation. Yet the desire to "return to normal," to get back in the church buildings, "is not just a misconception about traumatic survival; it is a dangerous move that threatens to elide the realities of traumatic suffering. This move also makes possible suffering's repetition."[72] If the coronavirus has taught us anything homiletically, it is that trauma should be a regular component of our preaching. We might also ask how our preaching in this century will be altered because of the pandemic. For years to come, COVID means that we will be preaching the "persistence of that event and the enigma of its remaining."[73]

A final homiletical implication gained from a trauma perspective is how we preach about the cross and resurrection event. Rambo suggests that "theologies of resurrection" are too often about the "erasure of wounds." Even though "the wounds return in the biblical narrative and feature centrally there, they are folded into interpretations that continually cover over the wounds."[74]

Jesus' appearance to Thomas affirms the importance of wounds in our processing of trauma. Thomas needs to see the wounds, to have the same experience as Mary Magdalene and the disciples, "We have seen the Lord!" to know the resurrection is true, but also to know that the trauma was true *and real.* Christian theology has taken up the cause to find meaning in the cross, and attention has been given to reimagining what "suffering on the cross" means. But it is also essential to cast suffering in the light of the time after the cross. "And yet conceiving the 'after' involves contending with the perplexing return of death within the sphere of life."[75] "A linear reading of cross and resurrection places death and life in a continuum; death is behind and life is ahead; life emerges victoriously from death. This way of reading can, at its best, provide a source of hope and promise for the future. But it can also gloss over the realities of pain and loss, glorify suffering, and justify violence."[76] Christian preaching knows that it cannot get to the resurrection without going through the cross. But it is not as knowledgeable when it comes to preaching the resurrection with the cross remaining.

FURTHER RESOURCES FOR PREACHING

Sancken, Joni. *Words That Heal: Preaching Hope to Wounded Souls.* Nashville: Abingdon Press, 2019.

Travis, Sarah. *Unspeakable: Preaching and Trauma-Informed Theology.* Eugene, OR: Cascade Books, 2021.

Wagner, Kimberly R. *Fractured Ground: Preaching in the Wake of Mass Trauma.* Louisville, KY: Westminster John Knox Press, 2023.

Conclusion

A conclusion to a book of this nature is more like an invitation. As the field of biblical studies and biblical interpretation expands and evolves, it will continue to be as diverse as interpreters themselves. Having an open stance toward Scripture, listening to the many meanings it prompts, and reading decentered voices can renew the biblical and homiletical imagination of even the weariest preacher. This book is then a summons to hold as invaluable in ministry the act and promise of conversation. The story of the Samaritan woman at the well (John 4:1–42) reminds us that conversation is essential to theology, to interpreting Scripture, and to a life of faith. Conversation is also, or at least should be, at the heart of preaching. Preaching is an inherently dialogical process and event—discourse between preacher, text, and congregation with the hope and prayer that the Spirit is overhearing and intervening when necessary. As isolating as the preaching life is wont to be, perhaps the interpretive approaches offered in this book can remain conversation partners and even inspire the search for new dialogue companions in our homiletical processes.

While this book focuses primarily on homiletical dividends from having a more expansive knowledge of the field of biblical interpretation, there are leadership and ministerial windfalls as well. Church leaders are about the business of shaping Christian identity, and the Christian life is shaped by preaching.[1] Just as there cannot be a single Latinx American approach to the Bible because of the variety of countries the designation represents, there is no single Christian approach to the Bible. An advantage, therefore, of deliberate engagement with multiple approaches to interpreting the Bible is welcoming discussion about and reflection on the specificities of Christian identity, especially to avoid "*unconscious* contextualization."[2] Our faith communities can and should be places that hold space for testimony. We all need practice in how to articulate, out loud, what kind of Christians we are and what sort of Christianity we espouse.[3] Equipping people to be able to share what it means for them to be Christian, owning their denominational, theological, and contextual specificities, can also address religious polarization. If "our identities—including our 'racial'/ethnic, class, sexual, gender, and even professional identities—are constructed and constantly hewed out dialogically in our ongoing and shifting social existence,"[4] how then is this also true for fashioning our Christian identity? Regularly engaging and lifting up contextual approaches to the reading of the Bible communicates that the development of Christian identity cannot happen in isolation. Part of identity formation is hearing what you are not. The forming of Christian identity is a dialogical enterprise.

Church leaders are also responsible for shaping, in part, the ethos of the community they serve. A key aspect of this process is being able to determine what biblical and theological tenets have been or will be foundational for a community's vision and mission. A greater awareness of viewpoints that shape biblical interpretation will lead to more definitiveness about a community's foundational beliefs. How can a preacher draw connections between the congregation's theological foundation and biblical themes? Often the preacher must challenge deeply embedded theological precepts within a community of faith for the sake of growth, even new birth. The role of preaching is critical in this ethos-forming activity. "Preaching sets the terms under which my congregation can justly be called a church. In each Sunday's sermon the church is reminded of who it is and to whom it is accountable. Preaching reiterates the identity and the mission of the church and enables Christians to discern and differentiate the story that forms and ever reforms the church as God's."[5]

Ferreting out a community's theology also means excavating our own. Engaging diverse perspectives in biblical interpretation places our own theological biases under the microscope. What do preachers keep as central to their theology? For example, Ellen Bernstein in *The Green Bible* puts forward the "Ten Commandments of Creation Theology."[6]

What, if any, of these commitments in a theology of creation do we hold dear? Or do we even have creation as a key component of what's at stake for us theologically? Conversation with interpreters representing contexts different from our own uncovers our rootedness and bares our blind spots.

For preachers, the perspectives rehearsed in this book also represent those we accompany in our ministry. Do the traumatized, the disabled, or the marginalized hear themselves in our sermons? Do persons who identify as LGBTQIA+ hear themselves in our sermons? Do the ecologically sensitive find themselves wondering whether the church, your church, cares about creation? Furthermore, listeners of our sermons carry out contextual hermeneutics all the time, yet how often do preachers acknowledge this truth? Employing these varied approaches in biblical scholarship can help preachers navigate with their listeners the challenging terrain of discussions about objectivity, subjectivity, and meaning making. People instinctively know the many contexts they bring to the act of interpretation, whether the text is a novel by Margaret Atwood or the Bible. They are also intuitively aware that all of life is an interpretive enterprise shaped by a plurality of contexts. We are constantly interpreting our surroundings, making sense of texts, whether written, situational, or persons, to arrive at next steps, decisions, or conclusions. A road sign requires deciphering so that the intended destination can be reached. At the same time, a ubiquitous belief is that the Bible can be interpreted without bias. "The Bible says" assumes an objectivity based on an ontological view of the authority of Scripture: the Bible is authoritative because it's the Bible. Such underlying suppositions operating within congregations and culture in general deserve and even demand scrutiny and negotiation, especially in a time when truth, falsehoods, and fake news have reinforced a society in denial about ideology. Perhaps our churches can host and hold safe spaces for conversation about and respect for the varied contexts that shape both faith and life, modeling dialogue and inquiry committed to deep listening, regard, and loving our neighbors as ourselves.

Theologically, this book can also contribute to understandings of the *imago Dei*, that is, the biblical claim that human beings are made in the image of God, "So God created humankind in his image, in the image of God he created them; male and female he created them" (Gen. 1:27).[7] Definitions and understandings of this biblical concept vary and are complex, but for the purposes here, to mirror the divine likeness of God also means to emulate God's actions and activity, to imitate God's nature and characteristics. Therefore, since God loves the world (John 3:16), the question for humans is, do we? And how do we? One way to exemplify the *imago Dei* is to regard others as God does; to love the diversity of humanity as God does; to love as God loves. Use and mention of varied approaches to interpreting the Bible presented in this book and then represented in our preaching are ways to embody our created nature and affirm created diversity.

Often in efforts to prove that the Bible is relevant, preachers are prone to diminution, especially when it comes to the hard truths that the Bible tells. We make soft correlates that we justify topically or thematically, but the associations lack both rigor and specificity. For example, the essence of Jesus' prayer at Gethsemane does not call for a sermon that says prayer is good for you. The betwixt-and-between experience of Latinx and Asian American communities is not the same as a pros-and-cons list for help in making a decision. Having an unbending boss at work does not mean you are experiencing colonization. The correlation of weight between the biblical circumstance and our context is a frequent homiletical misstep. The perspectives outlined in this book enflesh the stories and passages under scrutiny. It is not as easy to preach theological defaults when flesh and blood are at stake.

Finally, developing a greater knowledge base of biblical interpretation is a homiletical moral and ethical issue. When we ignore the diversity of interpretive lenses that can be brought to the Bible, we are then complacent in the work of dismantling the systemic *isms* that cause the very marginalization to which many of these voices give witness. "Existing on the margins of society and church provides a people with a special epistemological advantage, a certain way of knowing, that is fundamental to creating a just society and church."[8] In an increasingly polarized society where people and the churches they attend are retreating into denominational, theological, and ideological silos, how might preachers take on a commitment to amplification?[9] Rather than stake our ground over and against another, we give witness to what we have seen with our own eyes, "I have seen the Lord!" In an era that subtracts liberations, vilifies the unknown, justifies hateful speech, and validates merciless power, desperately needed is a generous homiletic. The preacher who listens to the real readers of Scripture embodies God's mercy and steadfast love.

Notes

Introduction

1. Mary F. Foskett and Jeffrey Kah-Jin Kuan, eds., *Ways of Being, Ways of Reading: Asian American Biblical Interpretation* (St. Louis: Chalice Press, 2006), xii.

2. Foskett and Kuan, xii.

3. Efrain Agosto, "Latino/a Hermeneutics," in *Hearing the New Testament: Strategies for Interpretation*, ed. Joel B. Green, 2nd ed. (Grand Rapids: Eerdmans, 2010), 365.

4. Francisco Lozado Jr., "Toward Latino/a Biblical Studies: Foregrounding Identities and Transforming Communities," in *Latino/a Biblical Hermeneutics: Problematics, Objectives, Strategies*, ed. Francisco Lozado Jr. and Fernando F. Segovia (Atlanta: SBL Press, 2014), 199.

5. Greg Carey, *Using Our Outside Voice: Public Biblical Interpretation* (Minneapolis: Fortress Press, 2020), 174.

6. Justo L. González, *Santa Biblia: The Bible through Hispanic Eyes* (Nashville: Abingdon Press, 1996), 15–16.

7. Carey, *Using Our Outside Voice*, 210.

8. Mona West, "The Raising of Lazarus: A Lesbian Coming Out Story," in *A Feminist Companion to John*, ed. Amy-Jill Levine, vol. 1 (Cleveland: Pilgrim Press, 2003), 143.

9. Elisabeth Schüssler Fiorenza, *Democratizing Biblical Studies: Toward an Emancipatory Educational Space* (Louisville, KY: Westminster John Knox Press, 2009), 3.

10. Bob Ekblad, *Reading the Bible with the Damned* (Louisville, KY: Westminster John Knox Press, 2005), xvi.

11. González, *Santa Biblia*, 33.

12. Carey, *Using Our Outside Voice*, 142.

Chapter 1: Literary/Narrative Approaches

1. Greg Carey, *Using Our Outside Voice: Public Biblical Interpretation* (Minneapolis: Fortress Press, 2020), 139.

2. Michal Beth Dinkler, *Literary Theory and the New Testament* (New Haven, CT: Yale University Press, 2019), 19.

3. Dinkler, 23.

4. Dinkler is quoting Irene De Jong, *Narratology and Classics: A Practical Guide* (Oxford: Oxford University Press, 2014), v.

5. David E. Aune, "Literary Criticism," in *The Blackwell Companion to the New Testament*, ed. David E. Aune (Chichester, UK: Wiley-Blackwell, 2010), 116–39.

6. Dinkler, *Literary Theory*, 7. See the overview in Carey, *Using Our Outside Voice*, 106–41.

7. Dinkler, *Literary Theory*, 17, 16. For a more detailed discussion of the inception of literary theory in biblical studies, see Dinkler's analysis, 16–18.

8. Dinkler, 6, 7.

9. A groundbreaking work in this regard is R. Alan Culpepper, *Anatomy of the Fourth Gospel* (Minneapolis: Fortress Press, 1987). See also David M. Rhoads, *Mark as Story: An Introduction to the Narrative of a Gospel*, 3rd ed. (Minneapolis: Fortress Press, 2012); Jeannine Brown, *The Gospels as Stories: A Narrative Approach to Matthew, Mark, Luke, and John* (Grand Rapids: Baker Academic, 2020); and Robert Alter, *The Art of Biblical Narrative* (New York: Basic Books, 2011).

10. Aune, "Literary Criticism," 133. See also Mark Allan Powell, "Narrative Criticism," in *Hearing the New Testament: Strategies for Interpretation*, ed. Joel B. Green, 2nd ed. (Grand Rapids: Eerdmans, 2010), 240–58.

11. Carey, *Using Our Outside Voice*, 107.

12. Meyer Abrams, *The Mirror and the Lamp: Romantic Theory and the Cultural Tradition* (Oxford: Oxford University Press, 1953), 6. See the full discussion in Dinkler, *Literary Theory*, 22–27.

13. Dinkler, *Literary Theory*, 23.

14. Dinkler, 33.

15. Dinkler, 24, 25. For Dinkler's full discussion of this taxonomy, see 22–27.

16. Dinkler, 25.

17. Dinkler, 28.

18. See *The International Standard Bible Encyclopedia*, vol. 4, ed. Geoffrey W. Bromiley (Grand Rapids: Eerdmans, 1998), s.v. "rhetorical criticism."

19. Dinkler, *Literary Theory*, 25.

20. Dinkler, 28.

21. Dinkler, 25, 29.

22. Dinkler, 33, 36.

23. Dinkler, 44.

24. Dinkler, 57.

25. Dinkler, 71, 75.

26. Dinkler, 101.

27. Dinkler, 103.

28. Dinkler, 107.

29. Dinkler, 108.

30. Dinkler, 191. Dinkler credits Mieke Bal with this phrase.

31. Carey, *Using Our Outside Voice*, 107.

32. Dinkler, *Literary Theory*, 194.

33. Powell, "Narrative Criticism," 245–46.

34. Portions of John 13–17, the Farewell Discourse, appear in the Easter season of the Revised Common Lectionary.

35. Gail O'Day, *Revelation in the Fourth Gospel: Narrative Mode and Theological Claim* (Minneapolis: Fortress Press, 1986).

36. This is a widely held position within Johannine scholarship to explain the Gospel's sectarian edge and dualistic imagery. For example, see the discussion in Gail R. O'Day, "John," in *The New Interpreter's Bible Commentary*, vol. 7 (Nashville: Abingdon Press, 1995), 647–51.

37. Carey, *Using Our Outside Voice*, 139.

38. W. Randolph Tate, "Literary Criticism," in *Handbook for Biblical Interpretation: An Essential Guide to Methods, Terms, and Concepts*, 2nd ed. (Grand Rapids: Baker Academic, 2012), 240–42, 241.

Chapter 2: Postcolonial Biblical Interpretation

1. R. S. Sugirtharajah, *Exploring Postcolonial Biblical Criticism* (Chichester, UK: Wiley-Blackwell, 2012), 13.

2. Sarah Travis, *Decolonizing Preaching: The Pulpit as Postcolonial Space* (Eugene, OR: Cascade Books, 2014), 2.

3. W. Randolph Tate, "Postcolonialism/Postcolonial Criticism," in *Handbook for Biblical Interpretation: An Essential Guide to Methods, Terms, and Concepts*, 2nd ed. (Grand Rapids: Baker Academic, 2012), 330.

4. Travis, *Decolonizing Preaching*, 2.

5. Travis, 3.

6. Travis, 2.

7. Sugirtharajah, *Exploring Postcolonial Biblical Criticism*, 1.

8. R. S. Sugirtharajah, *Postcolonial Criticism and Biblical Interpretation* (Oxford: Oxford University Press, 2002), 11, 33, 29.

9. Fernando F. Segovia, "John," in *A Postcolonial Commentary on the New Testament Writings*, ed. Fernando F. Segovia and R. S. Sugirtharajah (London: T&T Clark, 2007), 163.

10. R. S. Sugirtharajah, "Charting the Aftermath: A Review of Postcolonial Criticism," in *The Postcolonial Biblical Reader*, ed. R. S. Sugirtharajah (Malden, MA: Blackwell Publishing, 2006), 8.

11. Sugirtharajah, *Postcolonial Criticism and Biblical Interpretation*, 13.

12. Sugirtharajah, "Charting the Aftermath," 8.

13. Travis, *Decolonizing Preaching*, 4.

14. Sugirtharajah, "Charting the Aftermath," 7.

15. Tate, "Postcolonialism/Postcolonial Criticism," 329.

16. Sugirtharajah, "Charting the Aftermath," 7.

17. Sugirtharajah, *Postcolonial Criticism and Biblical Interpretation*, 11.

18. Warren Carter, "Postcolonial Biblical Criticism," in *New Meanings for Ancient Texts: Recent Approaches to Biblical Criticisms and Their Applications*, ed. Steven McKenzie and John Kaltner (Lousiville, KY: Westminster John Knox Press, 2013), 104.

19. Sugirtharajah, *Postcolonial Criticism and Biblical Interpretation*, 17.

20. Travis, *Decolonizing Preaching*, 4, 110, 47.

21. Fernando F. Segovia, "Biblical Criticism and Postcolonial Studies: Toward a Postcolonial Optic," in Sugirtharajah, *Postcolonial Biblical Reader*, 40.

22. Carter, "Postcolonial Biblical Criticism," 109.

23. Carter, 109.

24. Segovia, "John," 156.

25. Segovia, 168.

26. Segovia, 168.

27. John 3:1–17 occurs in the Revised Common Lectionary in Year A, Lent 2; Year B, Trinity Sunday; John 3:13–17 in Years A, B, and C, Holy Cross Sunday; John 3:14–21 in Year B, Lent 4.

28. See John 1:25, 26, 28, 31, 33; 3:22, 23, 26; 4:1, 2; 10:40. The focus of baptism is not on Jesus doing the baptism but on John and Jesus' disciples.

29. Travis, *Decolonizing Preaching*, 30, 38, 98, 48.

30. Travis, 99, 109.

31. *Merriam-Webster,* s.v. "politics," accessed August 31, 2022, https://www.merriam-webster.com/dictionary/politics.

32. Travis, *Decolonizing Preaching*, 5.

33. Travis, 23.

34. See Travis, 23–29.

35. Travis, 19.

36. Travis, 37.

Chapter 3: Feminist Interpretation

1. See Luise Schottroff, Silvia Schroer, and Marie-Theres Wacker, *Feminist Interpretation: The Bible in Women's Perspective* (Minneapolis: Fortress Press, 1998); Luise Schottroff and Marie-Theres Wacker, eds., *Feminist Biblical Interpretation: A Compendium of Critical Commentary on the Books of the Bible and Related Literature* (Grand Rapids: Eerdmans, 2012); Elisabeth Schüssler Fiorenza, ed., *Searching the Scriptures*, vol. 1, *A Feminist Introduction* (New York: Crossroad Publishing, 1993).

2. For a helpful summary of the rise and development of feminism, see Nyasha Junior, *An Introduction to Womanist Biblical Interpretation* (Louisville, KY: Westminster John Knox Press, 2015), 4–10.

3. Greg Carey, *Using Our Outside Voice: Public Biblical Interpretation* (Minneapolis: Fortress Press, 2020), 191. See also his summary, 191–95. *Mujeri* is a Spanish word for "woman." For a helpful explanation of *mujerista*, see

Ada Maria Isasi-Diaz, "Mujeristas: A Name of Our Own!!" https://www
.religion-online.org/article/mujeristas-a-name-of-our-own/. Another term
used in *mujerista* scholarship is "Latina American." See María Pilar Aquino,
"The Collective 'Dis-covery' of Our Own Power," in *Hispanic/Latino Theology:
Challenge and Promise,* ed. Ada María Isasi-Díaz and Fernando F. Segovia
(Minneapolis: Fortress Press, 1996), 241. A more detailed discussion of Latinx
interpretation is in chap. 5 of this book.

4. Wilda C. Gafney, *Womanist Midrash: A Reintroduction to the Women of the
Torah and the Throne* (Louisville, KY: Westminster John Knox Press, 2017), 6.

5. Gafney, 2n. Gafney also notes, "Yet womanism is also more complex, now
in its third (and perhaps fourth) wave, troubling its ancestral gender, ethnic, and
religious categories," 6.

6. Stephanie Buckhanon Crowder, *When Momma Speaks: The Bible and
Motherhood from a Womanist Perspective* (Louisville, KY: Westminster John Knox
Press, 2016), 21.

7. See Junior, *Womanist Biblical Interpretation,* 97–116.

8. Crowder, *When Momma Speaks,* 19. See also her history of womanist
development, 19–21, and overview of womanist biblical interpretation, 28–37.
See also Mitzi J. Smith, ed., *I Found God in Me* (Eugene, OR: Cascade Books,
2015), 17, for a summary of the term "womanist." See also Junior, *Womanist
Biblical Interpretation,* xi–xiv.

9. Amy-Jill Levine, "Feminist Criticism," in *The Blackwell Companion to the
New Testament,* ed. David E. Aune (Chichester, UK: Wiley-Blackwell, 2010),
156.

10. An excellent one-volume resource is *The Women's Bible Commentary,*
ed. Carol A. Newsom, Sharon H. Ringe, and Jacqueline E. Lapsley, 3rd ed.
(Louisville, KY: Westminster John Knox Press, 2012).

11. Crowder, *When Momma Speaks,* 36.

12. Linda M. Maloney, "The Pastoral Epistles," in *Searching the Scriptures,*
vol. 2, *A Feminist Commentary,* ed. Elisabeth Schüssler Fiorenza (New York:
Crossroad Publishing, 1994), 361.

13. Levine, "Feminist Criticism," 157.

14. See Joy A. Schroeder and Marion Ann Taylor, *Voices Long Silenced: Women
Biblical Interpreters through the Centuries* (Louisville, KY: Westminster John Knox
Press, 2022).

15. In the Revised Common Lectionary, John 4:5–42 occurs in Year A, Lent
3, as the second of four lections in a row from the Fourth Gospel. The other
passages are John 3:1–17 (Lent 2), 9:1–41 (Lent 4), and 11:1–45 (Lent 5). For
additional commentary on John 4:1–42, see Karoline M. Lewis, *John,* Fortress
Biblical Preaching Commentaries (Minneapolis: Fortress Press, 2014); and Gail
R. O'Day, "John," in Newsom, Ringe, and Lapsley, *Women's Bible Commentary,*
517–35.

16. Ruth Habermann, "Gospel of John," in Schottroff and Wacker, *Feminist
Biblical Interpretation,* 667.

17. There are two types of "I am" statements in the Gospel of John: the absolute "I am" statements without a predicate nominative: 4:26; 6:20; 8:24, 28, 58; 13:19; 18:5, 6, 8; and the "I am" statements with a predicate nominative: 6:35, 51; 8:12; 9:5; 10:7, 9, 11, 14; 11:25–26; 14:6; 15:1, 5.

18. Habermann, "Gospel of John," 669.

19. Habermann, 667.

20. Habermann, 666.

21. Habermann, 669.

22. The plight of the man born blind (John 9:1–3) is also assumed to be due to his sin or that of his parents.

23. Lindsay Hardin Freeman, *Bible Women: All Their Words and Why They Matter* (Cincinnati: Forward Movement, 2014).

24. Levine, "Feminist Criticism," 164.

25. 1 Cor. 14:34–35; 1 Tim. 2:8–15; Eph. 5:21–33; Gen. 1–3.

26. See Karoline M. Lewis, *SHE: Five Keys to Unlock the Power of Women in Ministry* (Nashville: Abingdon Press, 2016).

Chapter 4: African American Interpretation

1. Cleophus J. LaRue, "African American Preaching and the Bible," in *True to Our Native Land: An African American New Testament Commentary*, ed. Brian K. Blount, Cain Hope Felder, Clarice J. Martin, and Emerson B. Powery (Minneapolis: Fortress Press, 2007), 64.

2. For a brief history of African American biblical interpretation, see Esau McCaulley, *Reading While Black: African American Biblical Interpretation as an Exercise in Hope* (Downers Grove, IL: InterVarsity Press, 2020), 175–84.

3. C. Anthony Hunt, "African American Biblical Interpretation," in *Scripture and Its Interpretation: A Global, Ecumenical Introduction to the Bible*, ed. Michael J. Gorman (Grand Rapids: Baker Academic, 2017), 304.

4. Hunt, "African American Biblical Interpretation," 304.

5. Brian K. Blount, Cain Hope Felder, Clarice J. Martin, and Emerson B. Powery, introduction to *True to Our Native Land*, 2.

6. McCaulley, *Reading While Black*, 8.

7. Thomas Hoyt Jr., "Interpreting Biblical Scholarship for the Black Church Tradition," in *Stony the Road We Trod: African American Biblical Interpretation*, ed. Cain Hope Felder (Minneapolis: Fortress Press, 1991), 29.

8. Wilda C. Gafney, *Womanist Midrash: A Reintroduction to the Women of the Torah and the Throne* (Louisville, KY: Westminster John Knox Press, 2017), 2.

9. M. Shawn Copeland, *Enfleshing Freedom: Body, Race, and Being* (Minneapolis: Fortress Press, 2010), 19.

10. Allen Dwight Callahan, "The Gospel of John," in Blount, Felder, Martin, and Powery, *True to Our Native Land*, 189.

11. Mitzi J. Smith, *Insights from African American Interpretation* (Minneapolis: Fortress Press, 2017), 10.

12. Hoyt, "Interpreting Biblical Scholarship," 29.

13. LaRue, "African American Preaching," 64.

14. W. Randolph Tate, "African American Criticism," in *Handbook for Biblical Interpretation: An Essential Guide to Methods, Terms, and Concepts*, 2nd ed. (Grand Rapids: Baker Academic, 2012), 8.

15. Blount, Felder, Martin, and Powery, introduction to *True to Our Native Land*, 4.

16. Emerson B. Powery, "African American Criticism," in *Hearing the New Testament: Strategies for Interpretation*, ed. Joel B. Green, 2nd ed. (Grand Rapids: Eerdmans, 2010), 327.

17. James H. Cone, *The Cross and the Lynching Tree* (New York: Orbis Books, 2011), 158.

18. Cone, 118.

19. Hunt, "African American Biblical Interpretation," 301. See also Powery, "African American Criticism," 329.

20. Cone, *Cross and Lynching Tree*, 119.

21. For this discussion, see Cone, 149–50, 160.

22. Cone, 155.

23. Cone, xv.

24. John 18:1–19:42 is the Gospel reading for Good Friday in all three years of the Revised Common Lectionary.

25. One possibility is to follow the Narrative Lectionary for Year 4, which dedicates the third Sunday in Lent through Good Friday to the passion narrative in John. See https://www.workingpreacher.org/wp-content/uploads/2021/09/narrative_lectionary_john_2021-22_rev2.pdf.

26. Cone, *Cross and Lynching Tree*, 85.

27. Cone, 2.

28. Cone, 108.

29. Cone, 156.

30. The Greek term here specifically refers to a Roman cohort, approximately six hundred in number.

31. Cone, *Cross and Lynching Tree*, 156.

32. McCaulley, *Reading While Black*, 44.

33. John Thomas III, "The Seven Last Words of George Floyd," *Urban News*, April 14, 2021, https://theurbannews.com/spirituality/2021/the-seven-last-words-of-george-floyd/.

34. Cone, *Cross and Lynching Tree*, 122–23.

35. Mary's experience is poignantly captured in the African American spiritual "Were You There." See Callahan, "Gospel of John," 206.

36. For example, in the healing of the man ill for thirty-eight years in John 5 and the man born blind in John 9, both are healed of their ailments, but also offered abundant life in Jesus' community.

37. Cone, *Cross and Lynching Tree*, 3.

38. Cone, 2.

39. Cone, 21, 23.

40. Callahan, "Gospel of John," 207.

41. McCaulley, *Reading While Black*, 165.

42. Ibram X. Kendi, *How to Be an Antiracist* (New York: One World, 2019).

43. This is, of course, only a partial list of African Americans who have been killed at the hands of police and white supremacy. In the year after the murder of George Floyd on May 25, 2020, 229 Black people were killed by police. Khaleda Rahman, "Full List of 229 Black People Killed by Police since George Floyd's Murder," *Newsweek,* May 25, 2021, https://www.newsweek.com/full-list-229 -black-people-killed-police-since-george-floyds-murder-1594477.

44. Will Willimon, *Who Lynched Willie Earle? Preaching to Confront Racism* (Nashville: Abingdon Press, 2017), 89.

45. Willimon, 38.

46. Willimon, 39.

47. Willimon, 58.

48. McCaulley, *Reading While Black*, 165.

49. Cone, *Cross and Lynching Tree*, 75.

50. Willimon, *Who Lynched Willie Earle?*, 67.

51. Willimon, 75.

52. McCaulley, *Reading While Black*, 138.

53. See McCaulley, 152–62.

54. McCaulley, 144.

55. Especially as the sin of white supremacy leads to targeted massacres, for example, at Mother Emanuel African Methodist Episcopal Church, Charleston, South Carolina (June 17, 2015), and at a Tops supermarket in Buffalo, New York (May 14, 2022).

56. Willimon, *Who Lynched Willie Earle?*, 64.

57. Willimon, 108.

58. LaRue, "African American Preaching," 64.

59. Willimon, 109–10, 109.

60. Cone, *Cross and Lynching Tree*, xix.

61. Willimon, *Who Lynched Willie Earle?*, 41. See also Willie James Jennings, *The Christian Imagination: Theology and the Origins of Race* (New Haven, CT: Yale University Press, 2010), 79.

62. Willimon, *Who Lynched Willie Earle?*, 75.

Chapter 5: Latinx and Asian American Interpretation

1. The terms "Latin@" and "Latinx" are used as gender-neutral or nonbinary options, in place of "Latino/a." Throughout this chapter and in the literature, both Latino/a and Latinx are used. M. Daniel Carroll R. argues that Latino/ Latina should be the chosen designation, and not "Hispanic," which was used by the United States in the 1980 census but is far too broad to capture the

diversity of represented communities. M. Daniel Carroll R., "Latino/Latina Biblical Interpretation," in *Scripture and Its Interpretation: A Global, Ecumenical Introduction to the Bible*, ed. Michael J. Gorman (Grand Rapids: Baker Academic, 2017), 311.

2. Some knowledge of the terminological terrain of hyphenated existence is essential. While "American" is used predominantly in this book, the term "USian" is perhaps more accurate. "USian" is a demonym, "a word (such as *Nevadan* or *Sooner*) used to denote a person who inhabits or is native to a particular place." https://www.merriam-webster.com/dictionary/demonym. "USian," therefore, is "used to indicate that someone or something is of the United States of America. This is contrasted with 'American,' which technically means someone or something belonging to North or South America, including such disparate places as Guyana, Mexico, and Canada." https://www.urbandictionary.com/define.php?term=USian.

3. W. Randolph Tate, "Asian/Asian American Criticism," in *Handbook for Biblical Interpretation: An Essential Guide to Methods, Terms, and Concepts*, 2nd ed. (Grand Rapids: Baker Academic, 2012), 30.

4. Francisco Lozado Jr., "Toward Latino/a Biblical Studies: Foregrounding Identities and Transforming Communities," in *Latino/a Biblical Hermeneutics: Problematics, Objectives, Strategies*, ed. Francisco Lozado Jr. and Fernando F. Segovia (Atlanta: SBL Press, 2014), 191–92.

5. Lai Ling Elizabeth Ngan, "Neither Here nor There: Boundary and Identity in the Hagar Story," in *Ways of Being, Ways of Reading: Asian American Biblical Interpretation*, ed. Mary F. Foskett and Jeffrey Kah-Jin Kuan (St. Louis: Chalice Press, 2006), 70.

6. Rubén R. Dupertuis, "The Challenges of Latino/a Biblical Criticism," in Lozado and Segovia, *Latino/a Biblical Hermeneutics*, 135.

7. Carroll, "Latino/Latina Biblical Interpretation," 312.

8. Lozado, "Toward Latino/a Biblical Studies," 189.

9. Fernando F. Segovia, "Introduction: Aliens in the Promised Land," in *Hispanic/Latino Theology: Challenge and Promise*, ed. Ada María Isasi-Díaz and Fernando F. Segovia (Minneapolis: Fortress Press, 1996), 16.

10. Carroll, "Latino/Latina Biblical Interpretation," 316.

11. Carroll, 315, 317.

12. Ana Gonzalez-Barrera, "'Mestizo' and 'Mulatto': Mixed-Race Identities among U.S. Hispanics," Pew Research Center, July 10, 2015, https://www.pewresearch.org/fact-tank/2015/07/10/mestizo-and-mulatto-mixed-race-identities-unique-to-hispanics/.

13. Justo L. González, *Santa Biblia: The Bible through Hispanic Eyes* (Nashville: Abingdon Press, 1996).

14. Carroll, "Latino/Latina Biblical Interpretation," 317.

15. Eric Barreto, "Reexamining Ethnicity: Latina/os, Race, and the Bible," in Lozado and Segovia, *Latino/a Biblical Hermeneutics*, 87.

16. Barreto, 90.

17. Barreto, 91.

18. Foskett and Kuan, *Ways of Being*, xiii.

19. Frank M. Yamada, "Constructing Hybridity and Heterogeneity: Asian American Biblical Interpretation from a Third-Generation Perspective," in Foskett and Kuan, *Ways of Being*, 165–66. Adding to the complexity are questions about waves or phases—that is, who is being represented: first generation, immigrants or refugees, second and third generations who are United States or Canadian born.

20. K. K. Yeo, "Asian and Asian American Biblical Interpretation," in Gorman, *Scripture and Its Interpretation*, 324.

21. Yeo, "Biblical Interpretation," 330.

22. Matthew D. Kim and Daniel L. Wong, *Finding Our Voice: A Vision for Asian North American Preaching* (Bellingham, WA: Lexham Press, 2020), 13.

23. Yeo, "Biblical Interpretation," 326.

24. Andrew Yueking Lee, "Reading the Bible as an Asian American," in Foskett and Kuan, *Ways of Being*, 61–66.

25. Dupertuis, "Challenges," 135.

26. Jacqueline M. Hidalgo, "Reading from No Place: Toward a Hybrid and Ambivalent Study of Scriptures," in Lozado and Segovia, *Latino/a Biblical Hermeneutics*, 166.

27. Yeo, "Biblical Interpretation," 329.

28. Yamada, "Constructing Hybridity and Heterogeneity," 168.

29. Efrain Agosto, "Latino/a Hermeneutics," in *Hearing the New Testament: Strategies for Interpretation*, ed. Joel B. Green, 2nd ed. (Grand Rapids: Eerdmans, 2010), 356–57.

30. González, *Santa Biblia*, 80.

31. Hidalgo, "Reading from No Place," 167.

32. Cristina Garcia-Alfonso, "Latino/a Biblical Hermeneutics: Problematic, Objectives, Strategies," in Lozado and Segovia, *Latino/a Biblical Hermeneutics*, 151.

33. Agosto, "Latino/a Hermeneutics," 360–61.

34. In the Revised Common Lectionary, John 17 is spread out over the course of the three-year cycle as the Gospel reading for the Seventh Sunday of Easter: Easter 7, Year A, is John 17:1–11; Easter 7, Year B, is John 17:6–19; and Easter 7, Year C, is John 17:20–26.

35. See the discussion of the Paraclete in John in chap. 1.

36. See John 14:17, 19, 22, 27, 30, 31; 15:18, 19; 16:8, 11, 20, 21, 28, 33.

37. John 17:5, 6, 9, 11, 13, 14, 15, 16, 18, 21, 23, 24, 25.

38. Gilberto A. Ruiz, "'Out of Egypt I Called My Son': Migration as a Male Activity in the New Testament Gospels," in *Latinxs, the Bible, and Migration*, ed. Efraín Agosto and Jacqueline M. Hidalgo (Cham, Switzerland: Palgrave Macmillan, 2018), 96.

39. Ruiz, "Toward Latino/a Biblical Studies," 96.

40. Ruiz, 96.

41. Lozado, "Toward Latino/a Biblical Studies," 192.

42. Carroll, "Latino/Latina Biblical Interpretation," 316.

43. As M. Daniel Carroll R. notes, "The last four decades have witnessed overwhelming global economic, political, and ecological forces that are triggering the influx of millions of immigrants (both regular and undocumented) to the United States from Latin America, primarily from Mexico. For various reasons, this phenomenon has generated another layer of prejudice toward Latinos/as. The sense of national disdain is exacerbated by the fact that a large percentage of our people come from the poorer segments of society." "Latino/Latina Biblical Interpretation," 312–13.

44. Efraín Agosto and Jacqueline M. Hidalgo, introduction to *Latinxs, the Bible, and Migration*, 1.

45. Carroll, "Latino/Latina Biblical Interpretation," 320.

46. Agosto and Hidalgo, introduction, 11.

47. Agosto and Hidalgo, 13.

48. Carroll, "Latino/Latina Biblical Interpretation," 320.

49. Carroll, 316.

Chapter 6: Queer Interpretation

1. W. Randolph Tate, "Queer Theory," in *Handbook for Biblical Interpretation: An Essential Guide to Methods, Terms, and Concepts*, 2nd ed. (Grand Rapids: Baker Academic, 2012), 354.

2. See the groundbreaking volume edited by Deryn Guest, Robert E. Goss, Mona West, and Thomas Bohache, *The Queer Bible Commentary* (London: SCM Press, 2006).

3. Patrick S. Cheng, *Radical Love: An Introduction to Queer Theology* (New York: Seabury Books, 2011), 2–3.

4. Pamela R. Lightsey, *Our Lives Matter: A Womanist Queer Theology* (Eugene, OR: Pickwick Publications, 2015), xxii.

5. Laurel C. Schneider, "Queer Theory," in *Handbook of Postmodern Biblical Interpretation*, ed. A. K. M. Adam (St. Louis: Chalice Press, 2000), 206.

6. Lightsey, *Our Lives Matter*, 30.

7. Cheng, *Radical Love*, 4.

8. Cheng, 4.

9. Cheng, 4.

10. Cheng, 5.

11. Cheng, 6.

12. Cheng, 7.

13. Cheng, 8.

14. Cheng, 9. For a "genealogy" of queer theology, see 26–41.

15. Readers might recognize this as the Wesleyan quadrilateral.

16. Cheng, *Radical Love*, 4.

17. Linn Marie Tonstad, *Queer Theology: Beyond Apologetics* (Eugene, OR: Cascade Books, 2018), 2.

18. See also "Sexual Orientation, Gender Identity & Gender Expression," ReconcilingWorks: Lutherans for Full Participation, accessed September 1, 2022, https://www.reconcilingworks.org/resources/sogie/. In addition to having solid knowledge of these definitions, preachers should also familiarize themselves with the reasons for and uses of pronoun identification. See Laurel Wamsley, "A Guide to Gender Identity Terms," NPR, June 2, 2021, https://www.npr.org/2021/06/02/996319297/gender-identity-pronouns-expression-guide-lgbtq.

19. Schneider, "Queer Theory," 206.

20. Lightsey, *Our Lives Matter*, 27.

21. Cheng, *Radical Love*, 11.

22. Cheng, 11.

23. Cheng, 44–45.

24. Cheng, 73.

25. Tonstad, *Queer Theology*, 87.

26. Tonstad, 96.

27. Tonstad, 96.

28. Tonstad, 96–97.

29. Ken Stone, "Queer Criticism," in *New Meanings for Ancient Texts: Recent Approaches to Biblical Criticisms and Their Applications*, ed. Steven L. McKenzie and John Kaltner (Louisville, KY: Westminster John Knox Press, 2013), 156–57.

30. Mona West, "The Raising of Lazarus: A Lesbian Coming Out Story," in *A Feminist Companion to John*, ed. Amy-Jill Levine, vol. 1 (Cleveland: Pilgrim Press, 2003), 144.

31. Richard E. Goss, "John," in Guest, Goss, West, and Bohache, *Queer Bible Commentary*, 548.

32. Goss, 548.

33. Goss, 548.

34. Goss, 550.

35. See also the discussion of John's depiction of the "world" in chap. 5.

36. Goss, "John," 560.

37. Goss, 551.

38. Goss, 549.

39. Benjamin Perkins, "Coming Out, Lazarus's and Ours: Queer Reflections of a Psychospiritual, Political Journey," in *Take Back the Word: A Queer Reading of the Bible*, ed. Robert E. Goss and Mona West (Cleveland: Pilgrim Press, 2000), 198. This would also be true for the character of Nicodemus (John 3:3–4).

40. West, "Raising of Lazarus," 147.

41. Goss, "John," 552.

42. Goss, 553.

43. Goss, 554.

44. West, "Raising of Lazarus," 149.

45. Perkins, "Coming Out," 196–97, 199.

46. West, "Raising of Lazarus," 150.

47. Perkins, "Coming Out," 197, 200, 204.

48. West, "Raising of Lazarus," 154.

49. West, 157.

50. Goss, "John," 560.

51. Robert E. Goss, "The Beloved Disciple: A Queer Bereavement Narrative in a Time of AIDS," in Goss and West, *Take Back the Word*, 208.

52. Goss, 212.

53. Goss, 212.

54. Goss, "John," 561.

55. See Phyllis Trible's groundbreaking book, *Texts of Terror: Literary/Feminist Readings of Biblical Narratives* (Minneapolis: Fortress Press, 40th anniv. ed., 2022). West calls these texts "clobber passages." They include Sodom and Gomorrah (Gen. 19:1–28), "abominations" in Lev. 18:22 and 20:13, "degrading passions" in Rom. 1:26–28, and the vice lists in 1 Cor. 6:9 and 1 Tim. 1:10. West, "Raising of Lazarus," 145. See also the discussion in Tate, "Queer Theory," 354.

56. Tonstad, *Queer Theology*, 16–47.

57. Lightsey, *Our Lives Matter*, 49.

58. Tonstad, *Queer Theology*, 77.

59. Tonstad, 89.

60. Stone, "Queer Criticism," 156.

61. Tonstad, *Queer Theology*, 14.

Chapter 7: Ecological Interpretation

1. *The Green Bible* (San Francisco: HarperOne, 2008), I-15.

2. Ellen Bernstein, "Creation Theology: A Jewish Perspective," in *The Green Bible*, I-54–55.

3. Norman C. Habel, "Ecological Criticism," in Steven L. McKenzie and John Kaltner, *New Meanings for Ancient Texts: Recent Approaches to Biblical Criticisms and Their Applications* (Louisville, KY: Westminster John Knox Press, 2013), 44.

4. Francis Watson, "In the Beginning: Irenaeus, Creation and the Environment," in *Ecological Hermeneutics: Biblical, Historical, and Theological Perspectives*, ed. David G. Horrell, Cherry Hunt, Christopher Southgate, and Francesca Stavrakopoulou (London: T&T Clark International, 2010), 128.

5. Watson, 130.

6. Ellen F. Davis, "Knowing Our Place on Earth: Learning Environmental Responsibility from the Old Testament," in *The Green Bible*, I-58.

7. Habel, "Ecological Criticism," 47.

8. Ernst M. Conradie, "What on Earth Is an Ecological Hermeneutics? Some Broad Parameters," in Horrell, Hunt, Southgate, and Stavrakopoulou, *Ecological Hermeneutics*, 298.

9. Conradie, 298.

10. Conradie, 295.

11. Habel, "Ecological Criticism," 48. See also W. Randolph Tate, "Ecocriticism/Ecological Hermeneutics," in *Handbook for Biblical Interpretation: An Essential Guide to Methods, Terms, and Concepts*, 2nd ed. (Grand Rapids: Baker Academic, 2012), 134.

12. Habel, "Ecological Criticism," 48.

13. Tate, "Ecocriticism/Ecological Hermeneutics," 132.

14. Habel, "Ecological Criticism," 49.

15. David Horrell, introduction to Horrell, Hunt, Southgate, and Stavrakopoulou, *Ecological Hermeneutics*, 7.

16. Habel, "Ecological Criticism," 46.

17. The arrest of Jesus is part of John's passion narrative, which is the Revised Common Lectionary's Gospel reading for Good Friday in all three lectionary years (A, B, and C).

18. Richard Bauckham, "Reading the Synoptic Gospels Ecologically," in Horrell, Hunt, Southgate, and Stavrakopoulou, *Ecological Hermeneutics*, 70.

19. Bauckham, 70.

20. Bernstein, "Creation Theology," I-53.

21. Recall again that the "I am" statements are unique to the Gospel of John and have two grammatical constructions: the "I am" statements with a predicate nominative, 6:35, 51; 8:12; 9:5; 10:7, 9, 11, 14; 11:25–26; 14:6; 15:1, 5; and the "I am" statements without a predicate nominative, 4:26; 6:20; 8:24, 28, 58; 13:19; 18:5, 8.

22. J. Matthew Sleeth, "Introduction: The Power of a Green God," in *The Green Bible*, I-22.

23. Davis, "Knowing Our Place," I-59–60.

24. In the Gospel of John, sin is not a moral category but denotes separation from God, a severed relationship with God.

25. Tate, "Ecocriticism/Ecological Hermeneutics," 132, 135.

26. Davis, "Knowing Our Place," I-59.

27. Habel, "Ecological Criticism," 42.

28. Calvin B. DeWitt, "Reading the Bible through a Green Lens," in *The Green Bible*, I-25. DeWitt sets out six common obstacles to the care of creation: (1) "This world is not my home; I'm just passing through." (2) "There are too many worldly people out there doing environmental things." (3) "I don't want

to be an extremist or alarmist." (4) "I believe God gave us the job to do what we want with creation." (5) "People are more important than the environment." (6) "I disagree with what some environmentalists and scientists say will happen" (I-26–27).

29. Horrell, introduction, 3.
30. Sleeth, "Power of a Green God," I-22.
31. Watson, "In the Beginning," 129.
32. Brian McLaren, "Why I Am Green," in *The Green Bible*, I-45.
33. McLaren, I-44.
34. Horrell, introduction, 6.
35. DeWitt, "Green Lens," I-26.
36. Bernstein, "Creation Theology," I-55.
37. Archbishop Desmond Tutu, foreword to *The Green Bible*, I-13.
38. Watson, "In the Beginning," 138.

Chapter 8: The Bible and Disability

1. Anna Rebecca Solevåg, *Negotiating the Disabled Body: Representations of Disability in Early Christian Texts* (Atlanta: SBL Press, 2018), 4. For a more detailed history of disability studies, models, and approaches, see Solevåg's introductory chapter, 1–28.
2. Solevåg, 5.
3. Nyasha Junior and Jeremy Schipper, "Disability Studies and the Bible," in *New Meanings for Ancient Texts: Recent Approaches to Biblical Criticisms and Their Applications*, ed. Steven L. McKenzie and John Kaltner (Louisville, KY: Westminster John Knox Press, 2013), 22.
4. Candida R. Moss and Jeremy Schipper, introduction to *Disability Studies and Biblical Literature,* ed. Candida R. Moss and Jeremy Schipper (New York: Palgrave Macmillan, 2011), 2.
5. Moss and Schipper, introduction, 2.
6. Solevåg, *Negotiating the Disabled Body*, 5.
7. Junior and Schipper, "Disability Studies and the Bible," 22. See also Moss and Schipper, introduction, 3–4.
8. Junior and Schipper, "Disability Studies and the Bible," 22.
9. Jaime Clark-Soles, "John, First–Third John, Revelation," in *The Bible and Disability: A Commentary,* ed. Sarah J. Melcher, Mikeal C. Parsons, and Amos Yong (Waco, TX: Baylor University Press, 2017), 354. See also the discussion in Solevåg, *Negotiating the Disabled Body*, 5.
10. Junior and Schipper, "Disability Studies and the Bible," 22.
11. Junior and Schipper, 22–23.
12. Moss and Schipper, introduction, 4.
13. Solevåg, *Negotiating the Disabled Body*, 2.
14. Junior and Schipper, "Disability Studies and the Bible," 23.

15. Solevåg, *Negotiating the Disabled Body*, 7.

16. Solevåg, 3.

17. Amos Yong, *The Bible, Disability, and the Church* (Grand Rapids: Eerdmans, 2011), 8, 9.

18. Yong, 11.

19. Solevåg, *Negotiating the Disabled Body*, 10.

20. David M. Turner, *Disability in Eighteenth-Century England: Imagining Physical Impairment* (Hoboken: Taylor & Francis, 2012), 11.

21. Clark-Soles, "John," 336.

22. Solevåg, *Negotiating the Disabled Body*, 24, quoting Christian Laes, Chris F. Goody, and M. Lynn Rose, eds., *Disabilities in Roman Antiquity: Disparate Bodies a Capite ad Calcem* (Leiden: Brill, 2013), 8.

23. Junior and Schipper, "Disability Studies and the Bible," 26.

24. See Amy Jacober, *Redefining Perfect: The Interplay between Theology and Disability* (Eugene, OR: Cascade Books, 2017), 82–88, for a review.

25. Solevåg, *Negotiating the Disabled Body*, 19.

26. Elisabeth Schüssler Fiorenza, *Rhetoric and Ethic: The Politics of Biblical Studies* (Minneapolis: Augsburg Fortress, 1999), ix. See this discussion in Solevåg, 19.

27. Solevåg, *Negotiating the Disabled Body*, 22, 23, 24.

28. For a review of the history of the study of disability and the Bible, see Melcher, Parsons, and Yong, *Bible and Disability*, 1–14.

29. Yong, *Bible, Disability, and Church*, 13.

30. Clark-Soles, "John," 334.

31. Yong, *Bible, Disability, and Church*, 13.

32. Junior and Schipper, "Disability Studies and the Bible," 28.

33. John 9:1–41 is the Gospel lesson for Lent 4, Year A, in the Revised Common Lectionary.

34. Analyses of the healing stories in John 4:46–54 and 5:1–47 make for helpful comparisons when it comes to interpreting and preaching the healing of the man born blind. A full treatment of the other healings in John is beyond of the scope of this project, but references to them will be made in the interpretation of John 9.

35. Another angle on the story of the healing of the man in John 5, but one beyond the scope of this discussion, would bring the perspective of crip theory, a subset of disability studies. See Solevåg's discussion, *Negotiating the Disabled Body*, 133–52. Like the term *queer* in the LGBTQIA+ community, "*crip* represents a reclaiming of the derogatory term *cripple*. It is used as an inclusive term that expresses identity within disability culture and a resistance to regimes of normalcy." Solevåg goes on to explain that the term *crip* "reveals the impossible standard of the 'normal body' and shows how the idea of normal is dependent on its binary opposite, the abnormal," 133.

36. Colleen C. Grant, "Reinterpreting the Healing Narratives," in *Human*

Disability and the Service of God: Reassessing Religious Practice, ed. Nancy L. Eiesland and Don E. Saliers (Nashville: Abingdon Press, 1998), 74.

37. Yong, *Bible, Disability, and Church*, 51.

38. Clark-Soles, "John," 350.

39. Warren Carter, "'The blind, lame and paralyzed' (John 5:3): John's Gospel, Disability Studies, and Postcolonial Perspectives," in Moss and Schipper, *Disability Studies and Biblical Literature*, 145.

40. Carter, "'Blind, lame and paralyzed,'" 136. Carter also notes how "the disabled bodies of John's Gospel are signs, at least in part, of the destructive system of power that was the empire's food supply privileging elites and depriving nonelites of access to nutritionally adequate food," 143. Many disabilities, for example, were caused by mineral and vitamin deficiencies.

41. Carter, 144.

42. Solevåg, *Negotiating the Disabled Body*, 71.

43. See Solevåg's analysis of the Gospel of Mark, *Negotiating the Disabled Body*, 29–52. In Mark's healing stories, she specifically notes how the disabled person "props up" the protagonist. The term "narrative prosthesis" was coined by David T. Mitchell and Sharon L. Snyder, *Narrative Prosthesis: Disability and the Dependencies of Discourse* (Ann Arbor: University of Michigan Press, 2001).

44. Solevåg, *Negotiating the Disabled Body*, 54.

45. Solevåg, 66.

46. Grant, "Reinterpreting the Healing Narratives," 79.

47. Solevåg, *Negotiating the Disabled Body*, 63–64.

48. Grant, "Reinterpreting the Healing Narratives," 82.

49. Carter, "'Blind, lame and paralyzed,'" 130.

50. Solevåg, *Negotiating the Disabled Body*, 70.

51. Grant, "Reinterpreting the Healing Narratives," 81.

52. See Solevåg, *Negotiating the Disabled Body*, 70, who is quoting Grant, "Reinterpreting the Healing Narratives," 79.

53. Solevåg, 63–64.

54. Solevåg, 154.

55. Carter, "'Blind, lame and paralyzed,'" 130.

56. Solevåg, *Negotiating the Disabled Body*, 63.

57. For this discussion, see Yong, *Bible, Disability, and Church*, 56–57.

58. Yong, 56.

59. Grant, "Reinterpreting the Healing Narratives," 80–81.

60. Yong, *Bible, Disability, and Church*, 56.

61. Yong, 55.

62. Clark-Soles, "John," 338.

63. Clark-Soles, 339.

64. Grant, "Reinterpreting the Healing Narratives," 84.

65. Jacober, *Redefining Perfect*, 79.

66. Solevåg, *Negotiating the Disabled Body*, 73.

67. Carter, "'Blind, lame and paralyzed,'" 130, 145.

68. Grant, "Reinterpreting the Healing Narratives," 85.

69. Solevåg, *Negotiating the Disabled Body*, 159.

70. See Jacober, *Redefining Perfect*, 41–47, who also asks how disabled persons are "sinned upon," 44. See also the discussion about sin and disability in Nancy L. Eiesland, *The Disabled God: Toward a Liberatory Theology of Disability* (Nashville: Abingdon, 1994), 70–75.

71. Jacober, *Redefining Perfect*, 48.

72. Jacober, 66.

73. Jacober, 65.

74. Jacober, 16–17.

75. Jacober, 26–31.

76. Jacober, 20.

77. Clark-Soles, "John," 336.

78. Clark-Soles, 336.

79. Solevåg, *Negotiating the Disabled Body*, 157.

80. Eiesland, *Disabled God*, 100.

81. Eiesland, 107.

Chapter 9: The Bible and Trauma Theory

1. Shelly Rambo, *Spirit and Trauma: A Theology of Remaining* (Louisville, KY: Westminster John Knox Press, 2010), 3.

2. See the discussion in David G. Garber Jr., "Trauma Theory and Biblical Studies," *Currents in Biblical Research* 14, no. 1 (2015): 26.

3. Elizabeth Boase and Christopher G. Frechette, "Defining 'Trauma' as a Useful Lens for Biblical Interpretation," in *Bible through the Lens of Trauma*, ed. Elizabeth Boase and Christopher G. Frechette (Atlanta: SBL Press, 2016), 3.

4. Garber, "Trauma Theory," 28.

5. Rambo, *Spirit and Trauma*, 4.

6. Garber, "Trauma Theory," 28.

7. Rambo, *Spirit and Trauma*, 2.

8. Bessel van der Kolk, *The Body Keeps the Score: Brain, Mind, and Body in the Healing of Trauma* (New York: Penguin Books, 2015), 195.

9. Rambo, *Spirit and Trauma*, 2.

10. Rambo, 4. Here, Rambo narrates her conversation with Deacon Julius Lee of Greater St. Luke Baptist Church in New Orleans twenty-nine months after Hurricane Katrina. In his words, "The storm is gone, but the 'after the storm' is always here."

11. Van der Kolk, *Body Keeps Score*, 195.

12. Sarah Travis, *Unspeakable: Preaching and Trauma-Informed Theology* (Eugene, OR: Cascade Books, 2021), 21–22. See also van der Kolk, *Body Keeps Score*, 184–99.

13. Serene Jones, *Trauma and Grace: Theology in a Ruptured World* (Louisville, KY: Westminster John Knox Press, 2009), 12.

14. Garber, "Trauma Theory," 28.

15. See esp. van der Kolk, *Body Keeps Score*, whose work explores trauma's effects on the brain and body.

16. Rambo, *Spirit and Trauma*, 3, 4, 5, 7.

17. Travis, *Unspeakable*, 12.

18. Jones, *Trauma and Grace*, 13.

19. Jennifer L. Koosed, "Echoes of How: Archiving Trauma in Jewish Liturgy," in *Reading with Feeling: Affect Theory and the Bible,* ed. Fiona C. Black and Jennifer L. Koosed (Atlanta: SBL Press, 2019), 38.

20. Garber, "Trauma Theory," 37.

21. Dirk G. Lange, *Trauma Recalled: Liturgy, Disruption, and Theology* (Minneapolis: Fortress Press, 2010), 9.

22. Travis, *Unspeakable*, 33.

23. Garber, "Trauma Theory," 37.

24. Boase and Frechette, "Defining 'Trauma,'" 2.

25. Boase and Frechette, 4.

26. For example, Robert J. Schreiter examines biblical texts having in mind specifically the perspective of resilience, or "the capacity to live under and response to oppressive or violent situations over long periods of time." Schreiter, "Reading Biblical Texts through the Lens of Resilience," in Boase and Frechette, *Bible through the Lens of Trauma*, 193–207, quotation 193.

27. Travis, *Unspeakable*, 101–2.

28. Travis, 27.

29. Rambo, *Spirit and Trauma*, 5.

30. Boase and Frechette, "Defining 'Trauma,'" 6.

31. Boase and Frechette, 9.

32. Serene Jones describes the road to Emmaus story (Luke 24:13–43) as "a tale of trauma and survival." *Trauma and Grace*, 24.

33. Rambo, *Spirit and Trauma*, 82. Rambo dedicates a chapter in this book to "biblical witness in the Gospel of John," with specific attention to the testimony of Mary Magdalene and the Beloved Disciple. While some of this discussion is based on Rambo's analysis of John 20:11–18, additional interpretive possibilities, through the lens of trauma, provide the majority of the analysis. For Rambo's full discussion, see *Spirit and Trauma*, 81–110.

34. Rambo, 40.

35. Rambo, 40. See also the discussion in her chapter "Witnessing Trauma," particularly 37–44.

36. John 20:1–18 is the alternate Gospel reading for Easter Sunday all three years (A, B, C) in the Revised Common Lectionary.

37. Rambo, 82. The Beloved Disciple also sees the empty tomb, as does Peter, and believes, but his seeing of the empty tomb does not lead to an uttered

testimony. Rather, in chap. 21, witnessing the risen Christ on the seashore, he
then says, "It is the Lord!" (v. 7).

38. Rambo, *Spirit and Trauma*, 83.

39. See also Mark 15:40; Matt. 27:55–56; Luke 23:49; cf. Luke 8:1–3.

40. Mary Magdalene's role in the burial of Jesus varies in the Synoptic
Gospels. See Matt. 27:61, where she watches the burial, and 28:1, where she
goes to the tomb (without spices for anointing). In Mark, Mary Magdalene,
along with Mary the mother of James and Salome, "bought spices, so that they
might go and anoint him" (16:1). In Luke, she also watches the burial and then
brings spices to the tomb (23:55–24:11). Outside of John, only in Luke does she
testify to what she has seen, although it is not clear to what "this" refers, in "then
they remembered his words, and returning from the tomb, they told all *this* to
the eleven and to all the rest" (Luke 24:8–9; emphasis added).

41. Rambo, *Spirit and Trauma*, 83.

42. The light/darkness motif in the Gospel of John is discussed at length in
chap. 8, "The Bible and Disability."

43. Rambo, *Spirit and Trauma*, 91.

44. The only other occurrence of *klaiō* in the Gospel is in 16:20, when Jesus
is speaking his last words to his disciples, "Very truly, I tell you, you will weep
and mourn, but the world will rejoice; you will have pain, but your pain will
turn into joy."

45. Travis, *Unspeakable*, 25.

46. Rambo, *Spirit and Trauma*, 83.

47. Rambo, 98.

48. Rambo suggests that through the lens of trauma, the testimonies of both
Mary Magdalene and the Beloved Disciple are characterized by "distance and
disruptions" (96–99). In the narrative, they also embody true witness.

49. Rambo, 97.

50. Rambo, 3.

51. It is important to note that this detail of setting—a garden—is unique
to John's Gospel. Jesus' arrest, burial, and resurrection all take place in a garden,
again blurring the lines between death and life, between absence and presence
(John 18:1–11; cf. Matt. 26:26–56; Mark 14:32–51; Luke 22:39–54a).

52. Rambo, *Spirit and Trauma*, 87. Rambo focuses primarily on Mary's
inability to see, which then makes Mary's recognition of Jesus "different from
what we might expect." Rambo's discussion of witness, therefore, hinges primarily on a connection to sight. Yet, locating this story in the whole of John's narrative, this moment of realization recalls the Shepherd Discourse, as noted above.

53. Rambo, 87–88. Rambo argues that this "titular" claim is another example
of distancing and that "her moment of recognition is the reader's moment of
misrecognition" because the title has to be translated. The reader, however, if
following along in the narrative, would recall the words of Jesus from John 10 as
well as the calling of Lazarus by name to come out of the tomb.

54. Rambo, 91.

55. Mary is not alone in her unrecognition of the resurrected Jesus. In chap. 21, the disciples do not recognize Jesus until after their abundant catch of fish. Recognition happens in abundance.

56. From a Johannine narrative perspective, the injunction of Jesus points to the necessity of the ascension, still yet to happen. Jesus must now return to the Father (1:1; 14:2), from whence he came. The full extent of the incarnation will not find completion until the ascension. For John, the incarnation, crucifixion, resurrection, and ascension represent the fullness of Jesus' ministry.

57. Rambo, 27. See also Jay Geller, "Trauma," in *Handbook of Postmodern Biblical Interpretation*, ed. A. K. M. Adam (St. Louis: Chalice Press, 2000), 262.

58. Travis, *Unspeakable*, 57.

59. Rambo, *Spirit and Trauma*, 4.

60. Travis, *Unspeakable*, 3, 12.

61. Jones, *Trauma and Grace*, 92.

62. Shelly Rambo, *Resurrecting Wounds: Living in the Afterlife of Trauma* (Waco, TX: Baylor University Press, 2017), 149.

63. Rambo, *Resurrecting Wounds*, 145.

64. Rambo, 153.

65. Rambo, *Spirit and Trauma*, 110.

66. Rambo, 2.

67. Deanna Thompson, *Glimpsing Resurrection: Cancer, Trauma, and Ministry* (Louisville, KY: Westminster John Knox Press, 2018), 74.

68. Travis, *Unspeakable*, 40.

69. Travis, 61.

70. Travis, 4.

71. Travis, 74.

72. Rambo, *Spirit and Trauma*, 4.

73. Rambo, 156.

74. Rambo, *Resurrecting Wounds*, 11.

75. Rambo, 6.

76. Rambo, *Spirit and Trauma*, 143.

Conclusion

1. Will Willimon, *Leading with the Sermon: Preaching as Leadership* (Minneapolis: Fortress Press, 2020), 47.

2. Justo L. González, *Santa Biblia: The Bible through Hispanic Eyes* (Nashville: Abingdon Press, 1996), 16.

3. See Greg Carey, *Using Our Outside Voice: Public Biblical Interpretation* (Minneapolis: Fortress Press, 2020).

4. Timothy J. Sandoval, "How Did You Get to Be a Latino Biblical Scholar? Scholarly Identity and Biblical Scholarship," in *Latino/a Biblical Hermeneutics:*

Problematics, Objectives, Strategies, ed. Francisco Lozado Jr. and Fernando F. Segovia (Atlanta: SBL Press, 2014), 263.

5. Willimon, *Leading with the Sermon,* 16.

6. (1) "God as Creator"; (2) "Goodness"; (3) "Beauty"; (4) "Habitat: A Sense of Place"; (5) "Fruitfulness and Sustainability"; (6) "Interdependence, Relationship, and Community"; (7) "Language"; (8) "Boundaries"; (9) "Humanity's Place: Dominion and Service"; (10) "Shabbat: Time Out." Ellen Bernstein, "Creation Theology: A Jewish Perspective," in *The Green Bible* (San Francisco: HarperOne, 2008), I-52–56.

7. See also Gen. 5:1–3; 9:6; Rom. 8:29; 1 Cor. 11:7; 2 Cor. 3:18; 4:4–7; Col. 1:13–15; 3:10; Heb. 1:3; Jas. 3:9.

8. Kelly Brown Douglas, "Marginalized People, Liberating Perspectives: A Womanist Approach to Biblical Interpretation," in *I Found God in Me,* ed. Mitzi J. Smith (Eugene, OR: Cascade Books, 2015), 82.

9. Clarice J. Martin, "Womanist Interpretations of the New Testament: The Quest for Holistic and Inclusive Translation and Interpretation," in Smith, *I Found God,* 30–34.

Bibliography

Adam, A. K. M., ed. *Handbook of Postmodern Biblical Interpretation*. St. Louis: Chalice Press, 2000.

Agosto, Efrain. "Latino/a Hermeneutics." In Green, *Hearing the New Testament*, 350–71.

Agosto, Efrain, and Jacqueline M. Hidalgo, eds. *Latinxs, the Bible, and Migration*. Cham, Switzerland: Palgrave Macmillan, 2018.

Alexander, Michelle. *The New Jim Crow: Mass Incarceration in the Age of Colorblindness*. Rev. ed. New York: New Press, 2012.

Alter, Robert. *The Art of Biblical Narrative*. New York: Basic Books, 2011.

Aquino, María Pilar. "The Collective 'Dis-covery' of Our Own Power." In Isasi-Díaz and Segovia, *Hispanic/Latino Theology*, 240–58.

Aune, David E., ed. *The Blackwell Companion to the New Testament*. Chichester, UK: Wiley-Blackwell, 2010.

———. "Literary Criticism." In Aune, *The Blackwell Companion to the New Testament*, 116–39.

Barreto, Eric. "Reexamining Ethnicity: Latina/os, Race, and the Bible." In Lozado and Segovia, *Latino/a Biblical Hermeneutics*, 73–93.

Bauckham, Richard. "Reading the Synoptic Gospels Ecologically." In Horrell, Hunt, Southgate, and Stavrakopoulou, *Ecological Hermeneutics*, 70–82.

Bernstein, Ellen. "Creation Theology: A Jewish Perspective." In *The Green Bible*, I-51–57.

Black, Fiona C., and Jennifer L. Koosed, eds. *Reading with Feeling: Affect Theory and the Bible*. Atlanta: SBL Press, 2019.

Black, Kathy. *A Healing Homiletic: Preaching and Disability*. Nashville: Abingdon Press, 1996.

Blount, Brian K., Cain Hope Felder, Clarice J. Martin, and Emerson B. Powery. "Introduction." In Blount, Felder, Martin, and Powery, *True to Our Native Land*, 1–10.

Blount, Brian K., Cain Hope Felder, Clarice J. Martin, and Emerson B. Powery, eds. *True to Our Native Land*. Minneapolis: Fortress Press, 2007.

Boase, Elizabeth, and Christopher G. Frechette, eds. *The Bible through the Lens of Trauma*. Atlanta: SBL Press, 2016.

Boase, Elizabeth, and Christopher G. Frechette. "Defining 'Trauma' as a Useful Lens for Biblical Interpretation." In Boase and Frechette, *The Bible through the Lens of Trauma*, 1–26.

Brown, Jeannine. *The Gospels as Stories: A Narrative Approach to Matthew, Mark, Luke, and John*. Grand Rapids: Baker Academic, 2020.

Brown, Michael Joseph. *Blackening of the Bible: The Aims of African American Biblical Scholarship*. Harrisburg, PA: Trinity Press International, 2004.

Brown Douglas, Kelly. "Marginalized People, Liberating Perspectives: A Womanist Approach to Biblical Interpretation." In Smith, *I Found God in Me*, 80–86.

Callahan, Allen Dwight. "The Gospel of John." In Blount, Felder, Martin, and Powery, *True to Our Native Land*, 186–212.

Carey, Greg. *Using Our Outside Voice: Public Biblical Interpretation*. Minneapolis: Fortress Press, 2020.

Carroll R., M. Daniel. "Latino/Latina Biblical Interpretation." In Gorman, *Scripture and Its Interpretation*, 311–23.

Carter, Warren. "'The blind, lame and paralyzed' (John 5:3): John's Gospel, Disability Studies, and Postcolonial Perspectives." In Moss and Schipper, *Disability Studies and Biblical Literature*, 129–50.

———. "Postcolonial Biblical Criticism." In McKenzie and Kaltner, *New Meanings for Ancient Texts*, 97–116.

Cheng, Patrick S. *Radical Love: An Introduction to Queer Theology*. New York: Seabury Books, 2011.

Clark-Soles, Jaime. "John, First–Third John, Revelation." In Melcher, Parsons, and Yong, *The Bible and Disability*, 333–78.

Cone, James H. *The Cross and the Lynching Tree*. New York: Orbis Books, 2011.

Conradie, Ernst M. "What on Earth Is an Ecological Hermeneutics? Some Broad Parameters." In Horrell, Hunt, Southgate, and Stavrakopoulou, *Ecological Hermeneutics*, 295–313.

Copeland, M. Shawn. *Enfleshing Freedom: Body, Race, and Being*. Minneapolis: Fortress Press, 2010.

Crowder, Stephanie Buckhanon. *When Momma Speaks: The Bible and Motherhood from a Womanist Perspective*. Louisville, KY: Westminster John Knox Press, 2016.

Culpepper, R. Alan. *Anatomy of the Fourth Gospel: A Study in Literary Design*. Minneapolis: Fortress Press, 1987.

Davis, Ellen F. "Knowing Our Place on Earth: Learning Environmental Responsibility from the Old Testament." In *The Green Bible*, I-58–64.

DeWitt, Calvin B. "Reading the Bible through a Green Lens." In *The Green Bible*, I-25–34.

Dinkler, Michal Beth. *Literary Theory and the New Testament*. New Haven, CT: Yale University Press, 2019.

Dupertuis, Rubén R. "The Challenges of Latino/a Biblical Criticism." In Lozado and Segovia, *Latino/a Biblical Hermeneutics*, 133–49.

Eiesland, Nancy L. *The Disabled God: Toward a Liberatory Theology of Disability*. Nashville: Abingdon Press, 1994.

Eiesland, Nancy L., and Don E. Saliers, eds. *Human Disability and the Service of God: Reassessing Religious Practice*. Nashville: Abingdon Press, 1998.

Ekblad, Bob. *Reading the Bible with the Damned*. Louisville, KY: Westminster John Knox Press, 2005.

Felder, Cain Hope, ed. *Stony the Road We Trod: African American Biblical Interpretation*. Minneapolis: Fortress Press, 1991.

Foskett, Mary F., and Jeffrey Kah-Jin Kuan, eds. *Ways of Being, Ways of Reading: Asian American Biblical Interpretation*. St. Louis: Chalice Press, 2006.

Freeman, Lindsay Hardin. *Bible Women: All Their Words and Why They Matter*. Cincinnati: Forward Movement, 2014.

Gafney, Wilda C. *Womanist Midrash: A Reintroduction to the Women of the Torah and the Throne*. Louisville, KY: Westminster John Knox Press, 2017.

Garber, David G., Jr. "Trauma Theory and Biblical Studies." *Currents in Biblical Research* 14, no. 1 (2015): 24–44.

Garcia-Alfonso, Cristina. "Latino/a Biblical Hermeneutics: Problematic, Objectives, Strategies." In Lozado and Segovia, *Latino/a Biblical Hermeneutics*, 151–64.

Geller, Jay. "Trauma." In Adam, *Handbook of Postmodern Biblical Interpretation*, 261–67.

González, Justo L. *Santa Biblia: The Bible through Hispanic Eyes*. Nashville: Abingdon Press, 1996.

González, Justo L., and Pablo A. Jiménez. *Púlpito: An Introduction to Hispanic Preaching*. Nashville: Abingdon Press, 2005.

Gorman, Michael J., ed. *Scripture and Its Interpretation: A Global, Ecumenical Introduction to the Bible*. Grand Rapids: Baker Academic, 2017.

Goss, Robert E. "The Beloved Disciple: A Queer Bereavement Narrative in a Time of AIDS." In Goss and West, *Take Back the Word*, 206–17.

———. "John." In Guest, Goss, West, and Bohache, *Queer Bible Commentary*, 548–65.

Goss, Robert E., and Mona West, eds. *Take Back the Word: A Queer Reading of the Bible*. Cleveland: Pilgrim Press, 2000.

Grant, Colleen C. "Reinterpreting the Healing Narratives." In Eiesland and Saliers, *Human Disability and the Service of God*, 72–87.

Graves, Mike, and David Schlafer, eds. *What's the Shape of Narrative Preaching?* St. Louis: Chalice Press, 2008.

Green, Joel, ed. *Hearing the New Testament: Strategies for Interpretation*. 2nd ed. Grand Rapids: Eerdmans, 2010.

The Green Bible. San Francisco: HarperOne, 2008.

Guest, Deryn, Robert E. Goss, Mona West, and Thomas Bohache, eds. *The Queer Bible Commentary*. London: SCM Press, 2006.

Habel, Norman C. "Ecological Criticism." In McKenzie and Kaltner, *New Meanings for Ancient Texts*, 39–58.

Habel, Norman C., David Rhoads, and H. Paul Santmire, eds. *The Season of Creation: A Preaching Commentary*. Minneapolis: Fortress Press, 2011.

Habel, Norman C., and Peter Trudinger. *Exploring Ecological Hermeneutics*. Leiden: Brill Academic, 2008.

Habermann, Ruth. "Gospel of John." In Schottroff and Wacker, *Feminist Biblical Interpretation*, 662–79.

Hidalgo, Jacqueline M. "Reading from No Place: Toward a Hybrid and Ambivalent Study of Scriptures." In Lozado and Segovia, *Latino/a Biblical Hermeneutics*, 165–86.

Holbert, John. *Preaching Creation: The Environment and the Pulpit*. Eugene, OR: Cascade Books, 2011.

Horrell, David. "Introduction." In Horrell, Hunt, Southgate, and Stavrakopoulou, *Ecological Hermeneutics*, 1–12.

Horrell, David G., Cherryl Hunt, Christopher Southgate, and Francesca Stavrakopoulou, eds. *Ecological Hermeneutics: Biblical, Historical, and Theological Perspectives*. London: T&T Clark International, 2010.

Hoyt, Thomas, Jr. "Interpreting Biblical Scholarship for the Black Church Tradition." In Felder, *Stony the Road We Trod*, 17–39.

Hunt, C. Anthony. "African American Biblical Interpretation." In Gorman, *Scripture and Its Interpretation*, 298–310.

Isasi-Díaz, Ada María, and Fernando F. Segovia, eds. *Hispanic/Latino Theology: Challenge and Promise*. Minneapolis: Fortress Press, 1996.

Jacober, Amy. *Redefining Perfect: The Interplay between Theology and Disability*. Eugene, OR: Cascade Books, 2017.

Junior, Nyasha. *An Introduction to Womanist Biblical Interpretation*. Louisville, KY: Westminster John Knox Press, 2015.

Junior, Nyasha, and Jeremy Schipper. "Disability Studies and the Bible." In McKenzie and Kaltner, *New Meanings for Ancient Texts*, 21–37.

Kendi, Ibram X. *How to Be an Antiracist*. New York: One World, 2019.

Kenny, Amy. *My Body Is Not a Prayer Request: Disability Justice in the Church*. Grand Rapids: Brazos Press, 2022.

Kim, Eunjoo Mary. *Preaching and the Presence of God: A Homiletic from an Asian American Perspective*. Valley Forge, PA: Judson, 1999.

———. *Women Preaching: Theology and Practice through the Ages*. Eugene, OR: Wipf & Stock, 2009.

Kim, Matthew D., and Daniel L. Wong. *Finding Our Voice: A Vision for Asian North American Preaching*. Bellingham, WA: Lexham Press, 2020.

Koosed, Jennifer L. "Echoes of How: Archiving Trauma in Jewish Liturgy." In Black and Koosed, *Reading with Feeling*, 37–54.

Lange, Dirk G. *Trauma Recalled: Liturgy, Disruption, and Theology*. Minneapolis: Fortress Press, 2010.

LaRue, Cleophus J. "African American Preaching and the Bible." In Blount, Felder, Martin, and Powery, *True to Our Native Land*, 63–72.

Lee, Andrew Yueking. "Reading the Bible as an Asian American." In Foskett and Kuan, *Ways of Being, Ways of Reading,* 60–69.

Levine, Amy-Jill, ed. *A Feminist Companion to John.* Vol. 1. Cleveland: Pilgrim Press, 2003.

Lewis, Karoline M. *John.* Fortress Biblical Preaching Commentaries. Minneapolis: Fortress Press, 2014.

———. *SHE: Five Keys to Unlock the Power of Women in Ministry.* Nashville: Abingdon Press, 2016.

Lieu, Judith M., and Martinus C. de Boer, eds. *The Oxford Handbook of Johannine Studies.* Oxford: Oxford University Press, 2018.

Lightsey, Pamela R. *Our Lives Matter: A Womanist Queer Theology.* Eugene, OR: Pickwick Publications, 2015.

Lozado, Francisco, Jr. "Toward Latino/a Biblical Studies: Foregrounding Identities and Transforming Communities." In Lozado and Segovia, *Latino/a Biblical Hermeneutics,* 187–202.

Lozado, Francisco, Jr., and Fernando F. Segovia, eds. *Latino/a Biblical Hermeneutics: Problematics, Objectives, Strategies.* Atlanta: SBL Press, 2014.

Maloney, Linda M. "The Pastoral Epistles." In Schüssler Fiorenza, *Searching the Scriptures,* Vol. 2, *A Feminist Commentary,* 361–80.

Martin, Clarice J. "Womanist Interpretations of the New Testament: The Quest for Holistic and Inclusive Translation and Interpretation." In Smith, *I Found God in Me,* 19–41.

McCaulley, Esau. *Reading While Black: African American Biblical Interpretation as an Exercise in Hope.* Downers Grove, IL: InterVarsity Press, 2020.

McKenzie, Steven, and John Kaltner, eds. *New Meanings for Ancient Texts: Recent Approaches to Biblical Criticisms and Their Applications.* Louisville, KY: Westminster John Knox Press, 2013.

McLaren, Brian. "Why I Am Green." In *The Green Bible,* I-43–50.

Melcher, Sarah J., Mikeal C. Parsons, and Amos Yong, eds. *The Bible and Disability: A Commentary.* Waco, TX: Baylor University Press, 2017.

Meyers, Carol, Toni Craven, and Ross Shepard Kraemer, eds. *Women in Scripture: A Dictionary of Named and Unnamed Women in the Hebrew Bible, the Apocryphal/Deuterocanonical Books, and the New Testament.* Boston: Houghton Mifflin Harcourt, 2020.

Mitchell, David T., and Sharon L. Snyder. *Narrative Prosthesis: Disability and the Dependencies of Discourse.* Ann Arbor: University of Michigan Press, 2001.

Moore, Stephen D. "Postcolonialism." In Adam, *Handbook of Postmodern Biblical Interpretation,* 182–88.

Moss, Candida R., and Jeremy Schipper, eds. *Disability Studies and Biblical Literature.* New York: Palgrave Macmillan, 2011.

Moss, Candida R., and Jeremy Schipper. "Introduction." In Moss and Schipper, *Disability Studies and Biblical Literature,* 1–11.

Newsom, Carol A., Sharon H. Ringe, and Jacqueline E. Lapsley, eds. *Women's Bible Commentary*. 3rd ed. Louisville, KY: Westminster John Knox Press, 2012.

Ngan, Lai Ling Elizabeth. "Neither Here nor There: Boundary and Identity in the Hagar Story." In Foskett and Kuan, *Ways of Being, Ways of Reading*, 70–83.

O'Day, Gail R. "John." In Newsom, Ringe, and Lapsley, *Women's Bible Commentary*, 517–30.

———. *Revelation in the Fourth Gospel: Narrative Mode and Theological Claim*. Minneapolis: Fortress Press, 1986.

Perkins, Benjamin. "Coming Out, Lazarus's and Ours: Queer Reflections of a Psychospiritual, Political Journey." In Goss and West, *Take Back the Word*, 196–205.

Powell, Mark Allan. "Narrative Criticism." In Green, *Hearing the New Testament*, 240–58.

Powery, Emerson B. "African American Criticism." In Green, *Hearing the New Testament*, 326–49.

Rambo, Shelly. *Resurrecting Wounds: Living in the Afterlife of Trauma*. Waco, TX: Baylor University Press, 2017.

———. *Spirit and Trauma: A Theology of Remaining*. Louisville, KY: Westminster John Knox Press, 2010.

Reinhartz, Adele. "The Gospel of John." In Schüssler Fiorenza, *Searching the Scriptures*, Vol. 2, *A Feminist Commentary*, 561–600.

Rhoads, David M. *Mark as Story, An Introduction to the Narrative of a Gospel*. 3rd ed. Minneapolis: Fortress Press, 2012.

Ruiz, Gilberto A. "'Out of Egypt I Called My Son': Migration as a Male Activity in the New Testament Gospels." In Agosto and Hidalgo, *Latinxs, the Bible, and Migration*, 89–107.

Sancken, Joni. *Words That Heal: Preaching Hope to Wounded Souls*. Nashville: Abingdon Press, 2019.

Sandoval, Timothy J. "How Did You Get to Be a Latino Biblical Scholar? Scholarly Identity and Biblical Scholarship." In Lozado and Segovia, *Latino/a Biblical Hermeneutics*, 263–95.

Schade, Leah D. *Creation-Crisis Preaching: Ecology, Theology, and the Pulpit*. St. Louis: Chalice Press, 2015.

Schneider, Laurel C. "Queer Theory." In Adam, *Handbook of Postmodern Biblical Interpretation*, 206–12.

Schottroff, Luise, Silvia Schroer, and Marie-Theres Wacker, eds. *Feminist Interpretation: The Bible in Women's Perspective*. Minneapolis: Fortress Press, 1998.

Schottroff, Luise, and Marie-Theres Wacker, eds. *Feminist Biblical Interpretation: A Compendium of Critical Commentary on the Books of the Bible and Related Literature*. Grand Rapids: Eerdmans, 2012.

Schreiter, Robert J. "Reading Biblical Texts through the Lens of Resilience."
In Boase and Frechette, *The Bible through the Lens of Trauma,*
193–207.

Schroeder, Joy A., and Marion Ann Taylor. *Voices Long Silenced: Women
Biblical Interpreters through the Centuries.* Louisville, KY: Westminster John
Knox Press, 2022.

Schüssler Fiorenza, Elisabeth. *But She Said: Feminist Practices of Biblical
Interpretation.* Boston: Beacon Press, 1992.

———. *Democratizing Biblical Studies: Toward an Emancipatory Educational
Space.* Louisville, KY: Westminster John Knox Press, 2009.

———, ed. *Searching the Scriptures.* Vol. 1, *A Feminist Introduction.* New York:
Crossroad Publishing, 1993.

———, ed. *Searching the Scriptures.* Vol. 2, *A Feminist Commentary.* New York:
Crossroad Publishing, 1994.

Segovia, Fernando F. "Biblical Criticism and Postcolonial Studies: Toward
a Postcolonial Optic." In Sugirtharajah, *The Postcolonial Biblical Reader,*
33–44.

———. "Introduction: Aliens in the Promised Land." In Isasi-Díaz and
Segovia, *Hispanic/Latino Theology,* 15–42.

———. "John." In Segovia and Sugirtharajah, *A Postcolonial Commentary on the
New Testament Writings,* 156–93.

Segovia, Fernando F., and R. S. Sugirtharajah, eds. *A Postcolonial Commentary
on the New Testament Writings.* The Bible and Postcolonialism. London:
T&T Clark, 2007.

Sleeth, J. Matthew. "Introduction: The Power of a Green God." In *The Green
Bible,* I-17–24.

Smith, Mitzi J., ed. *I Found God in Me.* Eugene, OR: Cascade Books, 2015.

———. *Insights from African American Interpretation.* Minneapolis: Fortress
Press, 2017.

Solevåg, Anna Rebecca. *Negotiating the Disabled Body: Representations of
Disability in Early Christian Texts.* Atlanta: SBL Press, 2018.

Stone, Howard W., and James O. Duke. *How to Think Theologically.*
Minneapolis: Fortress Press, 1996.

Stone, Ken. "Queer Criticism." In McKenzie and Kaltner, *New Meanings for
Ancient Texts,* 155–76.

Sugirtharajah, R. S. "Charting the Aftermath: A Review of Postcolonial
Criticism." In Sugirtharajah, *The Postcolonial Biblical Reader,* 7–32.

———. *Exploring Postcolonial Biblical Criticism.* Chichester, UK: Wiley-
Blackwell, 2012.

———, ed. *The Postcolonial Biblical Reader.* Malden, MA: Blackwell Publishing,
2006.

———. *Postcolonial Criticism and Biblical Interpretation.* Oxford: Oxford
University Press, 2002.

Tate, W. Randolph. *Handbook for Biblical Interpretation: An Essential Guide to Methods, Terms, and Concepts*. 2nd ed. Grand Rapids: Baker Academic, 2012.

Thompson, Deanna. *Glimpsing Resurrection: Cancer, Trauma, and Ministry*. Louisville, KY: Westminster John Knox Press, 2018.

Tonstad, Linn Marie. *Queer Theology: Beyond Apologetics*. Eugene, OR: Cascade Books, 2018.

Travis, Sarah. *Decolonizing Preaching: The Pulpit as Postcolonial Space*. Eugene, OR: Cascade Books, 2014.

———. *Unspeakable: Preaching and Trauma-Informed Theology*. Eugene, OR: Cascade Books, 2021.

Trible, Phyllis. *Texts of Terror: Literary/Feminist Readings of Biblical Narratives*. 40th anniv. ed. Minneapolis: Fortress Press, 2022.

Tutu, Archbishop Desmond. Foreword. In *The Green Bible*, I-13–14.

van der Kolk, Besser. *The Body Keeps Score: Brain, Mind, and Body in the Healing of Trauma*. Reprint Edition. Penguin Publishing Group, 2015.

Watson, Francis. "In the Beginning: Irenaeus, Creation and the Environment." In Horrell, Hunt, Southgate, and Stavrakopoulou, *Ecological Hermeneutics*, 127–39.

West, Mona. "The Raising of Lazarus: A Lesbian Coming Out Story." In Levine, *A Feminist Companion to John*, 1:143–58.

Willimon, Will. *Leading with the Sermon: Preaching as Leadership*. Minneapolis: Fortress Press, 2020.

———. *Who Lynched Willie Earle? Preaching to Confront Racism*. Nashville: Abingdon Press, 2017.

Yamada, Frank M. "Constructing Hybridity and Heterogeneity: Asian American Biblical Interpretation from a Third-Generation Perspective." In Foskett and Kuan, *Ways of Being, Ways of Reading*, 164–77.

Yeo, K. K. "Asian and Asian American Biblical Interpretation." In Gorman, *Scripture and Its Interpretation*, 324–38.

Yong, Amos. *The Bible, Disability, and the Church*. Grand Rapids: Eerdmans, 2011.

Index

www.ingramcontent.com/pod-product-compliance
Lightning Source LLC
Chambersburg PA
CBHW020701080325
23155CB00030B/807